Absolute Crime P

Human Trafficking

Four Shocking Stories of Human Trafficking

ABSOLUTE
CRIME

By Reagan Martin and Tim Huddleston

Absolute Crime Books

www.absolutecrime.com

Table of Contents

About Us

Absolute Crime publishes only the best true crime literature. Our focus is on the crimes that you've probably never heard of, but you are fascinated to read more about. With each engaging and gripping story, we try to let readers relive moments in history that some people have tried to forget.

Remember, our books are not meant for the faint at heart. We don't hold back—if a crime is bloody, we let the words splatter across the page so you can experience the crime in the most horrifying way!

If you enjoy this book, please visit our homepage to see other books we offer; if you have any feedback, we'd love to hear from you!

Delivery of Death

The Shocking Story of the Ranong Human-Trafficking Incident

By Reagan Martin

Prologue

Thiry-two year old Ko Hla pulled his nineteen year old girlfriend closer, and managed a brave smile as they surveyed the small compartment of the refrigerated truck. He could feel the girl trembling at his side, her teeth chattering softly as if she had caught a chill, and he instinctively squeezed her tighter. He knew that she was not cold, only apprehensive, as she had been ever since leaving their native Burma to begin this long journey. Now, seeing the actual container of the truck, Ko was feeling anxious himself, although he was careful not to let his girlfriend know.

The truck compartment was tiny; much tinier than he had ever imagined it would be. Ko estimated that it couldn't measure more than 20 feet in length, and maybe 6 feet in width. Glancing around at the group of people who stood with him, he wondered how they would ever fit. The truck looked like it would have trouble carrying fifty people comfortably, let alone this crowd. Although Ko didn't know how many people were milling about with him, it certainly appeared to be a lot more than that, maybe even as many as 85 to 100.

The exact number of those about to embark on this passage with Ko Hla was 120, to be precise, and the young man was correct in his thinking. There was absolutely no way they would ever fit comfortably inside this small container.

Ko had not seen the driver of the truck, who would be responsible for transporting them to what they hoped would be good jobs and a better life, but a man and woman who had met them on the pier were there, walking amongst the waiting crowd, hastening them on.

'Hurry, hurry', they urged, 'climb up, get in. **Hurry**.'

The throng began to move towards the container, and Ko and his girlfriend were pushed along, inching closer and closer to the vehicle, which sat with its engine running. They pulled themselves up into the compartment, and as the rest of the waiting people struggled to climb aboard the two were forced to move further towards the front.

It was pitch black inside the truck box, and as Ko and his girl sat down, people kept coming, squeezing the couple closer and closer together until they were packed like sardines inside the stifling hot compartment.

Soon space in the tiny trailer ran out, and people were forced to sit on top of each other. Ko noticed a woman and child sitting near him, the woman holding the little girl on her lap, trying to soothe her. But no matter how much she cooed to the girl and whispered to her, Ko could see that it wasn't helping. The child appeared to be absolutely terrified.

After what seemed like an eternity the truck doors finally swung closed, and Ko could feel the vehicle begin to move. It shifted gears and slowly accelerated, rumbling along the invisible street outside.

The inside of the container was cloistered, terrifying in the inky black darkness, and sweltering hot. The sweat began to bead on Ko's forehead, and then seep out along the flesh of his arms. Soon it was running down his body in rivulets, soaking through his clothing and saturating his hair. It beaded up on the ends of each strand, dripping down into his eyes and creating a burning sensation that he was unable to relieve. The back of the truck was so tightly jammed with people it was nearly impossible for him to raise his hand just to wipe his eyes.

The others crammed into that tiny space were feeling the same way as Ko. Many of them desperately tried to shift position, an endeavor that was not only futile, but one which angered those sitting nearby. Several were beginning to cry, as their inability to do anything about their miserable situation increased their frustration. But it was what Ko heard next that really frightened him.

People were beginning to moan and wheeze, apparently gasping for air and unable to catch their breath. Several were muttering that they couldn't breathe. The little girl sitting on her mother's lap was crying and begging for help.

A dim glow began to penetrate the darkness as people lit lighters in a vain attempt to see. In the shadowy light, Ko could barely discern the appalling conditions, and the other anxious faces peering around. But it obvious that they were all in serious trouble, and he wondered how long would it be before panic set in.

In a desperate effort to get help, the people began to bang on the walls of the container, screaming for the truck driver to stop. They yelled and they pounded, using energy they couldn't afford to spare, but their calls went unheeded.

Although those inside the truck weren't aware of it, one man in their group had been provided with a cell phone and the number of the driver earlier in the evening. He quickly attempted to call the man, but he was panicked himself, and in the dark he fumbled with the phone, nearly dropping it. Willing himself to calm down, the man finally completed his call and was relieved when the driver answered. Nearly shouting, he begged him to stop the truck, telling him that there was no air inside and they were unable to breathe.

But the vehicle did not stop. It continued on its way, much to the dismay of those inside, and the moaning and gasping continued. And then, suddenly, there was a loud hissing noise, and cool, frosty air began to flow into the trailer. The driver hadn't stopped, but he had turned on the refrigeration unit, bringing immediate relief and joy to those trapped inside.

Ko said a mental prayer of thanks as he smiled down at his girlfriend. Then, unable to resist, he kissed the top of her head and nuzzled her sopping wet hair. The others inside began to laugh and to shout, delighted, happy, and blissfully unaware that the relief would be only temporary.

Chapter One

Ko Hla and his girlfriend, as well as the others riding in the back of the truck, were from the country of Burma, or Myanmar, a sovereign state in Southeast Asia. Their country had been under military control since 1962, and conditions there were harsh, as well as brutal. Well known for its inhumane treatment against its own people, the government of Burma subjected its citizens not only to horrendous living conditions, but also to genocide, child labor, slavery, repeated rapes of their women, and unbelievable poverty.

As a result of these gross human rights violations, and in an effort to escape them, thousands of Burmese people began to look elsewhere, hoping to find some place that would provide a better future for them. Between 1962, and 1988 a slow trickle of Burmese citizens migrated to other countries to start a new life.

But in 1988, when the Burmese Socialist Regime collapsed, it left its people out of work, destitute, and with no way to feed their families. In an effort to survive, millions more from the country of Myanmar were forced to flee, leaving all their worldly possessions to seek work elsewhere.

Although Burma is bordered by five different countries, Thailand, China, Laos, India, and Bangladesh, it was to Thailand that the majority of the Burmese people fled. The country was close by and reminiscent of home, and the border between Burma and Thailand was the Kra Buri River, making passage between the two countries easy. But more importantly, Thailand offered greater opportunities than Burma's others neighbors.

Many of these Burmese migrants entered Thailand in the city of Ranong, a small fishing port that bordered the Kra Buri River. Ranong was a center for the fishing and seafood industries, and in the year 2008, it had a population of 300,000. Nearly half of the city's residents were made up of Burmese migrants.

These migrants had come to Thailand hoping to find work and make a better life for themselves, and fortunately, for some, they would realize that dream. But for many others, the dream would quickly turn into a nightmare.

****

The government of Thailand, like most countries, was not receptive to welcoming millions of illegal immigrants crossing their borders. But unlike many other countries, Thailand had a great need for these alien bodies, and they knew it. The southern part of the country, with its beautiful beaches and balmy climate, was quickly becoming a major tourist destination, and growth in the area was rapid. And, as with any advancement, help was desperately needed.

There were jobs open for everyone; construction workers to build high rise hotels, and maids to clean them. People to work in the fish industry and on agricultural farms, ensuring there was enough food available to feed those who came to vacation. And of course women, young, sultry and sexy females, to pleasure those lonely souls who traveled there.

There was so much work in fact that the country couldn't provide enough manpower to fill the need. More and more often, the Thais would turn to migrants, both legal and illegal, to satisfy the demand. The migrants were hard working, discreet, and extremely cheap labor.

In December of 2004, when Thailand was hit by the great tsunami that resulted from the Indian Ocean earthquake, the southern part of the country was left in ruins. In the small resort areas around Ranong and Phuket, nearly 2600 people were killed, and the devastation was vast. Thailand desperately needed workers to re-build, and the Burmese migrants were eager to fill this need.

But without the Thai Government allowing them to legally enter the country, the people of Myanmar had no way to get in. Desperate to work and have money to feed their families, the majority of them were forced to turn to migrant brokers; men and women who offered to smuggle them into the country for a fee. To many of these desperate Burmese souls, finding a job broker seemed like a godsend. But in reality, it was not.

****

Whenever desperate circumstances arise, evil and greedy people are right there to seize the opportunity. They make their living preying on the vulnerabilities and desperate hopes of troubled and worried individuals, and the job brokers that many Burmese people turned to were no exception.

Migrant brokering is organized crime at its worst. A huge business, it generates millions of dollars in profit each year, and destroys just as many lives. It begins with the broker collecting a hefty fee, anywhere from 6,000 to 12,000 baht, (the equivalent of $180 to $360 U.S. dollars), to smuggle the illegal immigrant out of the country and secure him a job.

Since it was obvious that the typical migrant could never come up with that kind of money before he left the country, it was common for an arrangement to be agreed upon whereby the migrant would pay off his debt to the broker in installments. It seemed like the perfect arrangement, except that once the migrants were inside Thailand and working, they were quick to discover that they had blindly dug themselves into a hole they could never get out of.

Like others who desperately want something, and will agree to just about anything to get it, the migrants too rarely thought about the consequences of what they were agreeing to. They didn't consider the fact that they would be paid far less than the Thai natives, nor did they ever contemplate the price they were paying for their freedom. A broker's fee could be as high as 12,000 baht per person. For a lone migrant, this could take years to pay off, but for a family, with two or four children, the debt could last a lifetime.

But it was not only the broker that the migrant owed fees to, the police and military demanded a share of his wages as well. If the migrant didn't want to face criminal charges as an illegal alien, spend time in prison, be ordered to pay a fine, and then be deported back to his native country, he would have to pay.

Too late, many of those who came into the country illegally quickly realized that often their living conditions here were worse than they had been at home. After all the payouts, there was no money left to buy decent food, clothing or medical care.

The Burmese migrants also found that working conditions could be extremely harsh. For example, those who took jobs on a fishing vessel found that they were out to sea for thirty to forty days at a stretch, with only a three to five day respite in port. For this work, the migrant would be paid 3,000 to 6,000 baht per month, ($90 to $180 US dollars), while the Thai doing the same job on the same boat was paid double that. When he finally did get a few days off at home, he was too tired to spend it with his family, finding that he slept most of the time before returning to the ship.

Those migrants who went to work on farms found their working conditions pretty much the same as those on the fishing vessels. They worked long days, in sweltering heat, for very little money. The only exception was that they were allowed to be home each night.

Even worse than the fishing and farming industries were those who took jobs in factories. These migrants found themselves working in sweatshops, toiling from 12 to 14 hours each day for little more than $50 to $75 dollars a month.

There was another routine in their new country that greatly upset the immigrants; the practice of their new employers to confiscate their passports. Ordered to release them upon being hired, this action made it impossible for the migrants to quit their jobs, or leave the country, even if they wanted to.

After only a few weeks in their new home, many of those who had come seeking a brighter future found themselves saddled with debt, living in a foreign country, and missing the one thing that could get them home; their passports.

For Ko Hla and all the others riding in the small container of that miserable seafood truck, the chance that they were heading into this very same situation, although not thought about by them, was a distinct possibility.

Chapter Two

For all the ways that life in a new country had not lived up to the migrant's expectations, they found that they had a far bigger problem that overshadowed everything else. They were extremely vulnerable to human trafficking.

The distinction between migrant smuggling and human trafficking can often be difficult to determine. Very similar in nature, the only real difference between the two are consent, exploitation, and profit.

Those who hire a job broker and request to be smuggled out of a country are giving their consent. Their entire ordeal is supposed to end once their destination is reached. The profit made from this act comes from the transportation fee paid by the migrant, or by the money he pays to ensure his stay in the country.

On the other hand, a person who finds himself a victim of human trafficking is typically put into this position by means of force, threat, deception, coercion, or abuse of power. Upon reaching their destination, their ordeal doesn't end, but in fact is just beginning. They are no longer allowed any choices, are not free to leave, and are exploited by others in order for them to make a profit. These migrants might be forced to work as prostitutes, sold into slavery or forced labor, and even, at times, murdered to remove and sell their internal organs.

Although the two seem like different and distinct environments, migrant smuggling can quickly turn into human trafficking without the victim even knowing it. For instance, the migrant who paid the broker to smuggle him out of Burma and then took a job on the fishing boat is technically a smuggled immigrant. However, his being forced to work for abysmally low wages in order to pay off his broker's transportation fee is a form or coercion. Thus, without even being aware of it, this same man has moved from the category of smuggled migrant to human trafficking victim.

At other times trafficking is the intent all along, but the broker might approach the migrant and request a fee to gain his consent and trust. Because the immigrant initially agrees, it might look like a case of smuggling when all along the person was actually a victim of human trafficking.

On other occasions, the intent truly is only to smuggle, but if the broker finds himself faced with a lucrative opportunity to traffic the people instead, he will usually accept it. Human trafficking generates tens of billions of dollars in profits each year, and those involved in it are paid very well.

****

Victims of human trafficking include people of all ages and genders, but the vast majority of them are women. Seventy-nine percent of the estimated 2.5 million victims of human trafficking are being used for sexual exploitation. Many young girls are simply kidnapped off the streets and forced to work as prostitutes. But for others, their initiation into the world of the sex trade business came from people they knew and trusted.

One young Myanmar girl tells the story of being approached by a Burmese woman, who offered her a job as a maid in one of the fine hotels in the vacation town of Phuket. The woman assured her that the working conditions were exceptional, and she could expect to make a salary of about $950 a month, which included the tips she would receive from the rich people who stayed there. This was an astronomical amount of money for a poor Myanmar family, and the girl, only fifteen years old, readily accepted. She knew she could live on less than $200 a month, and would then be able to send the remaining money back to her struggling parents.

The fact that the job offer came from a female, and a fellow Myanmar, put the young girl at ease. She was not aware that most human traffickers prey on their own nationality, nor did she know that a large number of these predators are women who were once trafficked themselves. In an effort to escape their own plight, many females turn to the same crime that had victimized them in the first place.

When the young girl arrived in Thailand expecting to go to work in a hotel in Phuket she was instead kept in the city of Ranong and immediately locked away in small room for days on end. She saw no one, spoke to no one, and even her food, little more than a bowl of rice each day, was carefully placed on the floor just inside her door.

After about a week, the door to her prison opened and two men stood outside staring at her. One was young, while the other was a much older gentleman, probably somewhere in his mid to late sixties. The young man gestured at the girl, and then told the older man that the cost for 'opening a Burmese package' would be 13,000 baht. The old man nodded, handed the younger man a wad of bills, and then entered the room. The young man departed, pulled the door shut, and locked it from the outside.

Terrified, the young girl lay motionless as the older man ravished and raped her, panting and sweating as he nearly crushed her beneath him. When he was finally finished, the old man had laughed and then told her that 'opening a Burmese package' was a euphemism for having sex with a virgin Myanmar girl.

The ritual remained the same for the young girl month after month. She stayed locked away in the little room and was forced to have sex with dozens of strange men. Eventually her captors brought her out of her prison and put her to work in a Ranong brothel.

One day, seeing a rare opportunity, she fled from the house and flagged down a passing policeman. Begging him to help her, the officer instead returned her to the brothel, where she was stripped naked, repeatedly raped, and then viciously beaten.

This was not an unusual occurrence. Many of those in authority were blatantly corrupt and involved in the human trafficking trade for profit. Undoubtedly, the police officer who returned the girl to the brothel was paid handsomely by the owners to do so.

Had this policeman not been corrupt, the young girl's fate would not have been all that much better. She would certainly not have been viewed as a victim, but instead as criminal, guilty of illegal entry into the country, and most likely thrown in jail.

Before human trafficking became a well-known word, officials had little understanding of the difference between smuggling, trafficking, and migration. They viewed anyone in the country illegally, no matter how they came to be there, as criminals. Hauled into jail and placed in cells, they would be tried, sentenced to prison, given a stiff fine, and then deported back to their native countries. But most of the time their own country didn't want them back, and they were left with no money and no place to go. To many, their situation was hopeless.

But for the young prostitute who had tried to escape and failed, the isolation, humiliation, and terror eventually did its job. Just as her kidnappers knew she would, the girl yielding to her plight, and did what she was told. She never complained, cried, or tried to fight. And she never again attempted to escape.

But despite the fact that she was a model slave, turning tricks for her captors for nearly twelve hours a day, she received no money, and was never able to send her parents a dime. The other girls working with her explained that she would not make any money until she paid back what the brothel owners had spent to purchase her.

The young girl never saw the Burmese woman who had brought her to Thailand again, and her story, or ones exactly like it, are a dime a dozen. Some victims of human trafficking are never released from their bondage, often because death takes them first. Others, mainly the old or the injured, those who are of little value anymore, will sometimes be allowed to 'buy' their freedom. But the price is steep, and for thousands, nearly impossible to attain.

And for almost all of them, there is little hope of rescue. If this young girls parents ever managed to look for her, they would do so in Phuket, never knowing that they were looking in the wrong place. It was a standard ruse that the traffickers came to know worked very well.

****

For many of these slaves, their journey began the same way Ko Hla's had; in the small, cramped compartments of delivery trucks hired to carry them, and their hopes for a better future to destinations unknown.

Many had agreed to pay a price to leave their country, just like those now barreling down the highway trapped within the confines of the seafood trailer had. So, were Ko Hla and his group truly smuggled migrants, or were they too victims of human trafficking? The answer to that question remained to be seen.

Chapter Three

As the seafood truck continued to travel through the streets of Ranong, those locked inside did their best to ignore their uncomfortable surroundings. At least they could breathe a little easier now that there was finally some cool air flowing in from the refrigeration unit.

Other than some rustling and a few dry coughs, the container was mainly quiet, most of the migrants lost in thoughts of the life they were leaving behind and the new one they hoped to begin. Ko Hla sat with his eyes closed, concentrating on the events that had led him to this moment in time.

He had paid a migrant broker 12,000 baht to secure not only his entry into Thailand, but also a job in the resort city of Phuket, where major construction was underway. Phuket had been hard hit by the tsunami five years earlier, but it was a popular destination for tourists so re-building had been quick to begin. The new construction, however, was to be state of the art, not only beautiful, but also able to withstand the power of another tidal wave.

Hla, his girlfriend, and several others in the truck had made their way to Victoria Point, a Burmese town across the river from Ranong, where they were joined by more Myanmar citizens from other villages. All had paid a job broker to organize this trip for them.

Each was then hidden in the hold of a large cargo ship, another miserable and suffocating compartment, until sometime during the evening of April 8, 2008, when they sailed over to Thailand. The crossing had been uneventful, but upon docking, they were told they must remain in the cargo hold for another 24 hours. This announcement was greeted by sighs, moans, and outright curses.

Finally, around 7:00 pm, on April 9, 2008, they were allowed to leave the hold and come up on deck where they were immediately ushered onto the Choke Charoen fishing pier. A 10-wheeled truck, carrying a white, twenty foot long, unventilated seafood container was backed up to the pier, the doors of the trailer hanging open. Soon, a man and woman were urging them to get into the container, and to hurry.

Now, Ko Hla had been riding in that same container for the past hour. He knew the trip to Phuket would take about four hours total, and he hoped he could hang on that long. Already his legs were cramping, tingling, giving the annoying sensation that they had fallen asleep. He could hardly move an inch, his head throbbed and his back ached.

Someone nearby lit their lighter, casting an eerie glow in his immediate vicinity, and Ko noticed the woman with the child still on her lap. The little girl appeared to have fallen asleep, and Hla envied her. He wished he could fall asleep and escape this ride from hell.

The truck continued to rumble along, and those inside, although barely aware of the hiss of the compressor that released the cool, breathable air, knew immediately when it stopped working. There was no noise to indicate it, no bang or clank, but the hissing sound ceased abruptly, and there was no one who failed to notice it.

There were moans, and groans, and curses from the migrants, one lady muttering 'Oh, no," while another added sarcastically 'Well that's just great!'

The entire compartment seemed to rock and shimmy, as everyone came alert, moving and shifting, trying to figure out what had happened.

'Call the driver,' someone shouted.

But others in the truck were quick to veto the suggestion, telling the man with the phone, 'no, not yet'. They didn't want to make the driver angry, or seem like complainers. They thought it possible that he couldn't run the compressor the whole time, and if they just waited patiently, he'd turn it back on in a few minutes.

The others in the container didn't argue, and things quieted down for the moment. The man with the phone, who had taken it out and was ready to dial, took it as a silent agreement to wait.

****

Up front, sitting behind the wheel in the cab of the truck, thirty-eight year old Suchon Bunplong, like the migrants he was hauling, was also lost in thought. He was thinking about the events that led him to be driving a truck loaded with 120 illegal immigrants, and wishing that this trip were already over.

According to what he would later tell authorities, Suchon had been hired to do the job by a man named Damrong Phussadee, the owner of the seafood truck, and was paid 80,000 baht, ($2400 U.S. dollars) for the job. He had already received half of the payment up front, and was expected to receive the balance once he delivered his cargo in Phuket.

Suchon had been instructed to meet with a man and woman at the Choke Charoen fishing pier and pick up the truck there. The owner of the pier, Jirawat Sophapanworagul, was married to a woman who had been arrested in 1996 on a charge of human trafficking, although it is unclear whether Suchon knew about this. Also unclear was whether the man and woman he met on the pier were the Sophoapanworagul's.

Regardless, after leaving the pier with his human cargo, the woman had phoned him numerous times asking if everything was okay, and if he was sure the people had enough air in the back of the truck.

Suchon, although assuring her that all was well each time she called, was never the less annoyed to find that she continued to phone anyway. He didn't bother to tell her about the unexpected phone call he received, from one of the migrants in the back of the truck, telling him they couldn't breathe. Instead, he immediately turned on the trucks refrigeration system and all had quieted down.

But his thoughts were no longer on the woman and her phone calls, or the events that had led him to this moment in time. Instead, for the past twenty minutes, it had taken all of Bunplong's concentration just to negotiate the winding and twisting road in front of him. He had been driving for about an hour now, and the street was dark and narrow. Blind curves and numerous bends kept his eyes peeled open and his hands clenching the wheel. The man was nervous, on edge, and the fact that his cell phone just kept ringing didn't make matters any easier.

Whether Bunplong realized that the cooling system in the back of the truck had failed is not known. But what is known is that as the drive became more treacherous, and the phone continued to ring, he simply stopped answering it.

****

Within twenty minutes of the compressor shutting down, those trapped in the seafood container were sweating profusely, and beginning to have trouble catching their breath. The stench in the cramped compartment was enough to turn even the most hardened stomachs. It was the sickening sweet odor of human sweat, despair, and fear.

The little girl who lay in her mother's lap was no longer sleeping, and Ko Hla could hear her gasping for air. She kept pleading with her mother to help, telling her that she couldn't breathe. The mother was doing what she could, but she was crying and gasping for air herself.

Others in the truck were moaning and thrashing, crying out that they were burning up and unable to breath. Some began to shout, screaming at the man with the phone to call the driver. The man did so, repeatedly, but he never received an answer.

****

As Suchon maneuvered the truck through the inky black night, his cell phone continued to ring, shrilling out its tone every few minutes. Within a short amount of time, the ring tone remained constant, with barely a one second pause between each call. Frustrated, and with his nerves at their end, Suchon Bunplong reached over and turned the phone off.

****

Conditions in the cargo container of the truck were deteriorating rapidly. People appeared to be delirious now, calling out long phrases that made absolutely no sense. One man began struggling to get up, hitting and clawing at those jammed in next to him, shouting that he had vegetables in the garden that needed attending.

The heat in the container was brutal, blistering, and suffocating. People began peeling off their clothes, throwing them around, causing others to begin screaming at them in anger.

Soon, people were vomiting and choking, creating more vile odors to go along with the stench that was nearly unbearable. Within minutes the acrid smell of urine was added to the fray, permeating the air and making it difficult to even attempt a breath.

The little girl was no longer pleading for help, but her mother was moaning, and then wailing, squeezing the child tightly in her arms. Ko Hla was finding it hard to think straight or catch his breath. His temples pounded, and there were sounds and words and screams all jumbled in his head. He felt dizzy, disoriented and out of touch.

But suddenly, in the midst of all this chaos, Ko Hla heard the little girl's mother distinctly; and what he heard her saying chilled him to the bone.

"She's dead." The mother moaned, "My little girl is dead."

These words brought several in the truck to immediate attention. Now, more alert than they had been, they could hear others screaming and wailing about death and dying. The man with the cell phone was sobbing, telling the others that his calls were going directly to voice mail, an indication that the driver's phone had been shut off.

Ko Hla knew that they had to get out of this truck or they were all doomed. He began to bang against the side of the container, screaming for the driver to stop. Others joined in, pounding, banging, screaming at the top of their lungs, until the little white container was practically jostling from side to side.

****

Suchon Bunplong was startled to feel the truck container literally sway behind him, and then hear the screaming and banging emanating from it. He knew there was a problem back there, but he didn't know how serious it was. He was reluctant to stop for fear that it would arouse suspicion from passing motorists.

He continued to drive on, hoping that the migrants would settle down, but the ruckus from the container just continued to get louder and louder. Only a few miles up ahead there was a military checkpoint and Bunplong worried about approaching it. Typically, officials there needed only to see a 500 baht banknote and they would allow you to pass. But Suchon was certain that this time, the uproar in the container would not be ignored.

Reluctantly, he finally pulled his vehicle to the side of the road and got out. Moving to the back of the container, he unlocked the two doors and pulled them open. The migrants were packed so tightly inside that several of them tumbled out onto the pavement once the doors swung open.

Immediately, before Suchon could even look inside, more and more people were jumping from the container, gasping for air and falling to the ground. Finally, when it seemed all were out, Suchon peered into the compartment. What he saw made the blood in his veins run cold. He stared for a moment, horrified yet transfixed, and shivering despite the heat of the evening. And then he took off, abandoning the truck and its cargo, and fleeing the scene as fast he could.

Chapter Four

Around 10:30 pm, on the evening of April 9, 2008, the police of Ranong began receiving phone calls about a 10-wheeled white seafood truck abandoned on the side of the road in Village 3.

Responding to the scene, authorities were shocked by what they found. There were people milling all around the back of the truck, and several lying on the ground. Some looked to be unconscious, while others appeared delirious, crying and moaning, and sometimes even fighting while people tried to attend to them. Everyone seemed to be hysterical, and as the police approached, many rushed at them, all attempting to speak at the same time. While some officers tried to calm the frantic crowd, others climbed aboard the seafood container.

The first thing that hit them was the pungent odor coming from inside. It assaulted their senses, a foul, bitter combination of urine, body fluids, vomit, and dead fish. Shining their flashlights around, they were greeted by a grisly sight that stopped them in their tracks.

Clothing littered the floor and draped the bodies that were strewn all over the truck bed. They were sprawled in a jumble, contorted and twisted, some on top of each other, others remaining in the same seated position they had traveled in. One witness would later say that upon seeing the sight, he was immediately reminded of the aerial photos he had seen of the Jonestown Massacre in Guyana, the colored clothing scattered about and bodies piled on top of one another.

Stepping farther inside, the officers called to those lying motionless on the floor, nudging some with their feet, and bending to inspect others. There was no response from any of them, and it soon became apparent that those left inside were all dead.

There was a doctor on the scene, and the ambulances were called. Police watched as they rushed ten of those lying on the ground to area hospitals. Originally, when the news of the tragedy was made public, police would claim that 121 people had been in the truck. Days later, however, they would amend this count when they learned that one of those taken to the hospital was actually a Thai citizen who had fainted at the gruesome sight.

Incredibly, after the ambulances had left, police placed the other fifty-seven survivors under arrest and hauled them off to jail. Each was charged with illegally entering the country, and housed in prison cells overnight.

Inside the truck container authorities found fifty-four dead bodies; seventeen men, thirty-six women, and the eight year old little girl who had begged her mom for help.

****

After peering into the cargo bed of his truck and seeing the death and destruction that lay inside, Suchon Bunplong had panicked. With his heart pounding and his head spinning he immediately fled the scene, running as fast as his legs could carry him.

Eventually, he found a set of low-lying bushes and crawled under them, where he curled himself into a ball and hid. He was in a state of disbelief, shocked, panicked, and shivering with fear. By dawn he had calmed down enough to know that he couldn't hide forever. Emerging from the bushes, he walked to the nearest highway and began hitchhiking, quickly catching a ride to the Kapoe District.

Once there, he boarded a bus to Chumphon, getting off in the Lang Suan District. Later that evening he travelled to Nakhon Si Thammarat and then Bangkok, where he rented a motel room and watched the drama he was responsible for unfold on TV. He could hardly believe what he was hearing, and found it hard to look when they showed photos of the scene. Guilt ridden and deeply shamed, he wondered what to do.

****

Not surprisingly, when news broke of the suffocation deaths of fifty-four people being smuggled in the back of a sealed container, it produced a media storm throughout Thailand and the world. The story would go on to become the single most important event responsible for bringing the crime of human trafficking to the knowledge of the general public. It would also propel the country of Thailand into the spotlight, and create an international furor over the country's treatment of illegal immigrants.

Thai officials tried to do damage control by claiming that the country's problem with illegal aliens was one that the government was working on daily. In fact, they stressed, the Thai Prime Minister had recently suggested creating an Island Detention Center in the Adaman Sea to provide shelter for the illegals, and serve as a deterrent to others wanting to enter. As long as migrants avoided the legal channels needed to enter the country, they said, tragedies such as this were bound to happen.

****

Meanwhile, police continued their investigation into the entire event. The seafood truck had Ranong license plates, and was registered to Rungruengsup Limited Partnership. It was owned by a man named Damrong Phussadee, but as of now authorities had not located him, nor did they know the name of the driver who had also disappeared.

While some of the victims recuperated in the hospital and others languished in a jail cell, the dead were transported to a charity foundation where it was expected they would be buried in a pauper's grave.

To a country whose people are mostly Buddhist, this was devastating news to hear. Burial was the fate of any Buddhist who could not afford cremation at the temple, and it was not viewed as an honorable thing. To those who had survived the tragic event, the announcement felt like adding insult to injury.

****

On April 11, 2008, Damrong Phussadee, the owner of the seafood truck, presented himself to police and agreed to be questioned. He denied any involvement in the smuggling operation, and claimed that he knew nothing about his truck being used for such a criminal affair. Police did not believe him, and placed him under immediate arrest.

On the same day, those men and women who had been taken to jail were due in court. Standing before the bench, looking bedraggled and in a state of shock, the judge decided he needed more time to figure out what he should do with them. Refusing to make a decision on whether they would be tried as illegal immigrants or not, he ordered the group returned to their jail cells.

The next day the Burmese Minister Counselor Myint Soe travelled to Ranong and met with the country's Provincial Governor Kanchanapa Kiman. Kiman first offered Soe and the country of Myanmar her heartfelt condolences for the tragedy, and then quickly assured him that not only would the injured receive free medical care from her country, but she also promised that the truck owner would face 'strong charges' for his role in the crime.

Soe had been ordered by the Burmese government to come to Thailand and investigate the incident, and then report back to them. Soe knew his country was upset by what had happened, but he was also well aware of the Burmese government's reluctance to take back people arrested in Thailand for illegal entry. He was worried about what would happen to the survivors from the seafood truck.

Soe begged Kiman not to press charges against them, but Kiman was not in a position to comment on or give him an answer to his request. Later that day Soe paid a visit to some of the injured still in the hospital and the forty-six others who had been jailed.

That same afternoon, Burmese officials took a Myanmar job broker into custody. The man's name was Kyaw, but whether he was the broker who had arranged this particular trip was not known. Burmese officials declined to elaborate on his arrest.

****

On April 13, 2008, Region 8 Bureau Chief of Police Thani Tawitsri held a press conference that both stunned and angered the country, as well as the entire world.

Claiming that the fifty-four deaths could not be described as human trafficking, he told the news media that his investigation could only make a case against the truck driver, the truck owner, and the sixty-seven survivors of the tragedy.

He went on to say that he would be filing charges against the truck's driver and owner on two separate counts; bringing alien laborers into the Kingdom and giving them assistance and/or shelter, and with negligence causing death. He then added that he intended to charge the survivors with illegal entry into the country.

To say that the announcement caused anger would be an understatement. The news media, as well as the general public, were outraged. Hadn't those fifty-four people gone through enough? Now they were to be tried as common criminals too. People simply couldn't believe it.

On April 14th, in the hopes of doing damage control, the Department of Special Investigation, (DSI), Police Sergeant Suchart Wongananchai, commander of foreign affairs and the international crime office, held his own press conference.

If Thailand refused to enforce the anti-trafficking laws, he said, then the assets of those involved in this case should be confiscated. His investigation had found that these trafficking rings could make 'not less than 100,000 baht' per trip. In his opinion, he continued, when you had this type of 'forced labor smuggling', into a country, and that generated tremendous amounts of money, then it should be viewed as an 'economic crime'. If it were viewed as such, then those involved could, and should, have the freezing of their assets imposed on them.

Suchart had learned that the Burmese victims had paid the job broker anywhere from 8,000 to 12,000 baht each for the job. He also knew that once they were in the country they would be required to pay Thai Government Officials another 10 to 20 baht each, every day, to look the other way.

Suchart emphasized that the survivors should be witnesses in the case, and not 'accused persons', and that the Thailand Government should be responsible for their expenses while they were staying in the country.

Although most people agreed with what Suchart had to say, few of them thought it would actually happen. Needless to say, Thai authorities and Government officials didn't agree with, nor were they happy or impressed by his speech.

****

Meanwhile, Suchon Bunplong, the driver of the truck, was spending his days wandering around in the Sanam Luang district, wracked with guilt. He could not believe that he was responsible for so many people dying, and it haunted him.

Every evening he would return to his hotel room and watch the news coverage of the disaster, becoming more and more depressed and despondent each time he did. But once his mind began to clear and he could think again, little by little his depression was overcome by another emotion; fear.

Bunplong, although not a high-ranking member of any group, was well aware of how far reaching the human trafficking enterprise went. He knew about the billions of dollars that was involved in the trade, and it scared the hell out of him.

What would stop the other members of the ring from killing him to keep him quiet, he wondered? After all, he was the key to the incident, the one who could name names, times, and places. He had the ability to interrupt their entire operation, if not destroy it, within a matter of minutes.

He grappled with the thought of which was worst; becoming a snitch and going to prison, or ending up dead? He knew he would have to make a decision, and he wanted to make it before he was caught. In his search for an answer, he turned to his family. His sister had always helped him in the past; perhaps she could do so again.

Calling her several times, speaking for hours on end, the two siblings finally decided that the best course of action was for Suchon to turn himself in. His sister volunteered to speak to officials and set up the surrender, and Suchon readily agreed.

Chapter Five

The Thai police may have been unable to enforce the anti-trafficking laws in the case of the 120 Burmese migrants, but they certainly knew that human trafficking existed. Not only did it exist, but it was also a major criminal enterprise that was flourishing within their country.

Authorities suspected that the human trafficking ring responsible for bringing the Burmese workers into the country was the Je Ngor gang (Elder Sister Ngor). This was one of five influential groups known to be involved in the human trafficking of Burmese job seekers in the Ranong area. The five groups were a combination of both Thai and Burmese brokers who bribed Thai officials to avoid arrest.

The human trafficking problem in Thailand was more complex than anyone realized at the time. Although all genders were involved, the majority of those being trafficked were young females, brought in for the purpose of working in the sex trade. Some of these girls were forced into prostitution, but for others, those with beautiful faces and lush bodies, the fate was sometimes worse. Many were sold to individual owners, who used them for such things as personal sex slaves, maids, and occasionally punching bags.

But not all of those being trafficked were from other countries, nor were they only female. Many Thai girls, as well as young males from here and abroad, were also forced to work in the sex trade, and compelled to do so by the same means used on others; fear, force, deception, and coercion.

While traffickers could be brutal and heartless, they apparently had no regard for the age of their victims either. Some of those forced to work in the sex trade were as young as six years old. In fact, Thailand's Health System Research Institute reported that even today, 40% of those working as prostitutes in the country of Thailand are children.

One lone female forced into prostitution can provide her trafficker with an income of $250,000 a year. Many will continue to work the girl for years and years, but for others, the sale of the girl outright to another 'pimp' can bring a small fortune in itself. Many 'pimps' (and they are not always men, are more than willing to pay a handsome price for a girl who has already had 'her spirit broken'.

For people forced into a situation, like being ordered to work as a prostitute, the initial reaction for many is defiance. Most, in the beginning, will seize any opportunity to challenge and rebel against their captor. They will fight and defy them at every turn, and desperately try to escape from them. It can take a long time, and a lot of hard work, to transform the woman into a meek and tolerant individual, willing to do just about anything to remain in her captor's good graces.

The methods used to achieve this goal are often ugly and violent, but extremely effective. It requires the systematic brainwashing of an individual, produced by fear, negligence, and savage, brutal beatings. The captor needs the girl to view him as her only means of survival. She must depend on him for all things; the food she eats, the clothes she wears, even the very air she breathes. Traffickers call this 'breaking her spirit', and it is a task that many people find exceptionally distasteful. Thus, potential buyers are willing to pay a tremendous amount of money to have it already done for them.

Like everything else, the sex slave trade in Thailand has ripple down effects. It is a major source of the rampant increase in HIV and AIDS to the country, where an estimated 610,000 people die every year from the deadly disease. And of course, it is also a key contributor to the spread of those less lethal STD's such as gonorrhea and herpes.

From the sex trade to being sold into forced labor, both male and female trafficking victims experience a lot of the same living and working conditions, and they are always held in a financial bondage of indebtedness too.

There were a number of complications that hindered the investigations of human trafficking cases. Prosecuting them was extremely difficult, partly because of the blatant internal corruption of many of those in law enforcement, the government, and the military. A vast number of members from these organizations were not only content to turn their heads and look the other way, but several were also directly involved in the crimes, and took an active role in the incidents.

There was also the fact that most Thai people were not sympathetic to the migrant workers' plight. To the natives, the immigrants were a source of cheap labor who invaded their country and stole work that rightfully belonged to them. Compassion for those held prisoner in a slave trade was not an emotion most Thais were willing to give.

In addition, the lack of understanding as to what human trafficking actually was, and the difficulty in identifying authentic trafficking victims made the crime harder to discern. And the courts of Thailand were well known for their inability to recognize human rights based labor abuse cases.

The main question authorities faced in determining charges against those responsible in the suffocation deaths of the fifty-four Burmese migrant workers was; were they being trafficked at all, or simply smuggled? Where was the evidence of exploitation? Apparently there wasn't any, or at least none that they could prove. Police were quick to point out that each person inside that truck had willingly volunteered to come to Thailand.

****

Even though the police were doing everything in their power to convince the public that this was simply a case of illegal entry that turned tragic, Thailand's Foreign Minister, Noppadon Pattama, urged them to view the incident not only as an illegal immigration crime, but also one of human trafficking. He demanded that those involved be arrested, and that the survivors of the tragedy be treated like victims rather than criminals.

But it did little good. The police eventually announced that it didn't matter what the circumstances might appear to be, there was no way to prove it was a case of human trafficking, and so therefore, it would not be considered as such.

Of course, there was another reason that authorities might have preferred this to be a case of smuggling rather than trafficking. Treating the incident as a smuggling case would speed up the survivor's deportations, and therefore not allow them to stay in Thailand and claim compensation.

****

On April 15, 2008, Suchon Bunplong finally turned himself into the police and confessed his role in the Burmese deaths tragedy. He claimed that it was Damrong Phussadee, the owner of the truck, who had arranged the entire thing and ordered him to pick up the migrants at the Choke Chareon fishing pier.

Bunplong also confessed that he failed to acknowledge his ringing cell phone and the migrants banging on the sides of the truck because he was trying to concentrate on his driving. He then admitted that although he was guilt ridden by what had happened, he had turned himself in mainly out of fear of the other members of his group that he described as a human trafficking ring.

Even with Bunplong's confession in hand, police still insisted they could not bring charges of human trafficking.

Chapter Six

By April 16, 2008, police had three people in custody for the 'death truck incident', as it had come to be called, and had issued warrants for four more. Those already in jail were Suchon Bunplong, the driver, Damrong Phussadee, the truck owner, and Jirawat Sophapanworagul, the owner of the Choke Charoen fishing pier. Police had yet to arrest Weera Dum Yingyaud, Chalhermchai Waritjanpleng, his wife, Panchalee Chusuk, and Supat Phothong. By the very next day, April 17, 2008, authorities had picked up both Waritjanpleng and Yingyaud.

Yingyaud claimed to be Suchon Bunplong's accomplice, and to have ridden with him in the cab of the truck. He told authorities that he had been on several human trafficking runs with Bunplong and was paid 10,000 baht for each one. In addition, he also confessed to being the one who actually opened the truck doors after the migrants had begun screaming and banging on the walls. But he, just like Bunplong, had fled the scene when he realized what had happened, and had gone into hiding.

Waritjanpleng, who was thirty years old and the nephew of Jirawat Sophanworagul, the owner of Choke Charoen fishing pier, had voluntarily turned himself in to the Ranong Provincial Police. Authorities charged him with 'having knowledge of foreigners illegally entering the country, providing them with shelter so they could avoid arrest, and carelessness leading to their deaths'.

Chalhermchai claimed that his uncle, Jirawat, was not involved in the incident, nor was Chalhermchai's wife Panchalee. Police believed Panchalee to be the woman who had counted the Burmese migrants before they entered the truck, and had issued a warrant for her arrest.

Chalhermchai went on to say that he was given 20,000 baht by Supat Phothong to let human traffickers use his uncle's pier. Supat, he continued, was a labor broker who took orders from native Thai's for Burmese workers. Although Chalhermchai denied any other wrongdoing in the case, police did not believe him. They had been told by others in custody that it was Chalhermchai who had not only let the traffickers use the pier, but had also been responsible for loading the migrants into the truck. In addition, he had been the one to open and close the doors on a warehouse, allowing the truck to enter and exit the building.

After learning of what had happened to the migrants in the back of the truck, Chalhermchai claimed that he had fled to Pattani, alone, and hidden there until turning himself in. He insisted that after the news broke he and his wife had gone their separate ways, even though she had no involvement in the smuggling of the workers. Although he would not tell authorities where she was, he promised them that he would have his wife turn herself in the next day.

But instead of waiting, thirty-five year old Panchalee Chusuk contacted authorities that same day and offered to surrender, telling them that she was eager to prove her innocence.

Questioned at the home of Ranong Police Chief Apirak Hongthong, Panchalee denied counting the migrants as they boarded the truck, and only admitted to keeping track of those passing through the warehouse where the truck was parked. She had only done this, she stressed, so she could prepare packets of food for them.

She then insisted that neither her husband, nor his uncle, Jirawat, had any involvement in the crime. She and her husband had fled to Pattani after hearing the news, simply out of fear, and had hidden out at the home of a relative. Authorities did not fail to note that this statement completely contradicted her husbands, who had said that he and his wife had gone their separate ways.

Now, eight days after the discovery of the fifty-four dead migrants, police had all the suspects involved in custody, save one. Only Supat Phothong, the thirty-four year old man believed to be the broker who brought the Burmese migrants to Thailand, had escaped capture. The others were held at the Ranong prison, awaiting trial, and denied bail.

****

The public and the news media were still clamoring for those involved in the 'death truck incident' to be tried on human trafficking charges, but by mid-April, that idea was put to rest once and for all.

On April 21, 2008, Immigration Police Commander Lieutenant General Chatchaw al Suksomjit held a press conference to confirm that there was not enough evidence to charge those involved with human trafficking. Instead, he told the waiting press, the six Thai Nationals would be charged with death by negligence, and could receive a maximum sentence of ten years for each person who had died.

Although disgusted, the public took some consolation in the thought that those responsible might be serving 540 years in prison.

****

At the same time, the survivors of the tragedy were learning the penalty they would have to pay for having been subjected to such a horrific ordeal.

Fourteen were minors, and immediately deported back to Burma without facing charges, and two others were not charged because they were still trying to recover in a Thailand hospital. That left the remaining fifty to face trial and learn their punishment.

All were convicted of illegal entry into the country, and sentenced to ten days in jail. In addition, each was fined 2,000 baht, and deported back to Burma.

But they had gotten off easy. After all, they were facing a two-month prison sentence, but the sympathetic Thailand courts only gave them ten days.

Afterword

The suffocation death of 54 Burmese migrant workers in the back of a sealed container did more to bring attention to the crime of human trafficking, and the plight of its victims, than any other event before or since. Yet human trafficking continues to occur, and it remains a thriving business.

There have been several discrepancies in the story told by both survivors of this tragedy and those who witnessed it. Some say the people were forced to ride in the truck standing up, and that the truck had been stopped on the side of the road for more than an hour, waiting for a military checkpoint to close for the night. Others claimed that the air conditioner did not break down, but that Bunplong shut it off deliberately, while some insist the driver never unlocked the doors before he fled. They claim it was nearby villagers who heard their cries for help and finally freed them.

The entire truth of what actually happened in the 'Ranong Human Trafficking Death Truck' will probably never be known. All one can hope is that those 54 people did not die in vain, and that their death can be a lesson the world will learn from.

Those who had high hopes that the perpetrators of the ordeal might receive as much as 540 years in prison, as authorities had claimed, were sorely disappointed when the trials were complete. Of the seven people suspected to be involved in the 'death truck incident', five were convicted of gross negligence and breaking immigration laws and their sentences ran as follows:

Damrong Phussadee, who owned the truck, received ten years in prison.

Jirawat Sophapanworagul, the owner of the Choke Charoen fishing pier received a sentence of six years.

Chalhermchai Waritjanpleng, who received money for letting the traffickers use his uncle's pier, was sentenced to nine years.

Panchalee Chusuk, Chalhermchai's wife, who counted the migrants as they boarded the truck, originally received a six-year term, but this was subsequently reduced to three years.

Suchon Bunplong, the driver of the truck who disregarded the immigrant's pleas for help, received twelve years, but because he had confessed to trafficking illegal aliens, his sentence too was cut in half and he was ordered to do six years.

It is unknown whether authorities ever picked up Supat Phothong; the alleged broker who procured the 120 Burmese migrants for those Thai's who had ordered them. Although police had issued a warrant for his arrest, as of this date, he apparently has not been tried.

The same goes for Weera Dum Yingyaud, who was arrested, but as of now has not gone to trial. It could not be determined whatever became of him, and it is possible that he was released from custody and the charges against him dropped.

Three of those convicted were immediately released from jail after posting bond of 200,000 to 400,000 baht. They will remain free pending their appeal.

All of the survivors from the back of the seafood truck were repatriated back to Burma, and to the majority of the public, the feeling that they got a raw deal ran high. Even the National Human Rights Commission publicly stated that Thailand had 'treated them shabbily.'

Although what happened to those 120 victims was tragic, they were but a drop in the bucket when you consider the tens of thousands of Burmese migrants who enter Thailand each year. Many of these other migrants die too; the only difference is that their deaths didn't make headlines.

In November of 2007, seven Burmese migrants, along with their Thai taxi driver, were killed when the taxi they were riding in crashed during a high-speed chase to avoid arrest.

In December of that same year, twenty-two more died when the rickety old boat they were being smuggled in capsized, and all were drowned.

Another seven drowned in January while trying to make the crossing into Thailand.

There are many such stories from numerous other illegal immigrants, all of them simply trying to find a better life.

Leaders from all over the world now regularly meet to discuss ways to crack down on human trafficking and prosecute those involved in it. There are conferences held, papers written, seminars attended, and speeches made, yet the answer on how to end this trade is as elusive as ever.

Thailand itself set June 6, 2008 as 'D-Day' for human trafficking, issuing a stricter law on that date to supersede their more lenient one against trafficking. But the crime still exists in the country.

It might be that no matter what governments and law enforcement agencies try to put in place to quell this barbaric crime, it may never be enough. For it is only when all individuals come to realize that every human being has worth, value, and the right to be treated with decency and respect that the human trafficking trade will cease to exist.

Bibliography

www.ide.go.jp/Englis/Publish/Download/DP/pdf/257.pdf

myanmarhumantrafficking.gov.mm/content/faqs

www.worldvision.com.au/issues/humantrafficking

www.phuketgazette.net/news/details.asp?fromsearch=yes&id=6397&search=driver

Phuketwan.com/tourism/horror-of-human-trade-54-die-in-Phuket-bound-container/

www.thedailybeast.com/newsweek/2008/04/12/lured-into-bondage.html

www.phuketgazette.net/archives/articles/2008/article6402.html

teakdoor.com/Thailand-and-asia-news/27304-54-burmese-job-seekers-soffocate-ranonh-2.html

www.foxnews.com/printer_friendly_wires/2008apr16/0,4675,thailandsuffocationdeaths,00.html

whatismatt.com/the-trouble-with-burmese-migrants/

www.alipac.us/f12/thailand-driver-thai-truck-tragedy-surrenders-105877/

www.upi.com/top_news/2008/04/16/surrender-in-deadly-migrant-smuggling/upi-566312083771

www.asiaviews.org/regional-news-a-specials-report/22393-reportalias3568?tmpl=component&print=1&page=

teakdoor.com/593322-postl.html

www.phuketgazette.net/news/savedf.php?ref=20131170538&id=19835

phuketgazette.net/archives/articles/2008/articles6241.html

updates.theworldrace.org/?filename=all-about-thailand

www.humantrafficking.org/countries/thailand

www.mekongmigration.org/mmn/?p=70

www.no-trafficking.org/content/press_rooms_pdf/thai%20fm%20said_mcot_17_08.pdf

www.cesd.soc.cmu.ac.th/2012/en/news.php?cmd=detail&id=2039

usatoday30.usatoday.com/news/world/2008-04-09-2857217462-x.htm

twocircles.net/node/66132

Slaves of Berkeley

The Shocking Story of Human Trafficking In the United States

By Tim Huddleston

Chapter 1: An Accidental Death

It was the afternoon before Thanksgiving Day in 1999, and longtime Berkeley resident Marcia Poole was driving down Bancroft Way when she noticed four Indian men hauling what appeared to be a rolled-up rug out of a rundown apartment building. Maybe it was the rushed, nervous manner of the men, maybe it was the way the rug they carried was sagging in the middle, or maybe it was just a gut feeling, but Ms. Poole knew that something about what she was witnessing was very, very wrong. She slowed down and watched the men as they opened the door to a van that was parked at the curb. As they loaded their cargo inside the back of the vehicle, Ms. Poole's suspicions were confirmed when she saw a leg dangle out from beneath the folds of their bundle. At that point, she did what most people in her position never would have done—she stopped her car, got out and walked over to confront the men.

As she marched towards the van, she saw another group of men holding onto a teenage Indian girl dressed in traditional baggy and colorful garb, her black hair pulled into a braid. She was crying and screaming, trying to pull away from the men as she pleaded with them in a language Ms. Poole did not understand. But she didn't need an interpreter to know that the men were trying to force the young girl into the van against her will. Ms. Poole rushed over and planted herself in front of the open doors and demanded that the men stop what they were doing and release the girl. The men froze and looked back at her for a moment in uncertainty. None of them seemed accustomed to taking orders from a woman, especially a woman they didn't know. One of them stepped forward, and the others parted to let him through. He was a heavy-set, round-faced Indian man in his early sixties, and he was clearly the one in charge. He glared at Ms. Poole with the confidence and intimidating demeanor of a man who always gets his way. "Go away," he said. "This is a family affair."

Marcia Poole may have been brave, but she wasn't stupid. She was extremely outnumbered and didn't want her rescue attempt to end up with her being tossed into the back of the van as well. She did as the man commanded and moved away, but not before she noticed that the body the men had thrown inside the van was moving. It was another young Indian girl and Ms. Poole could now see that what she had mistaken for a rug was actually the girl's clothing, and she had been completely wrapped up in it. She must have been knocked out when she was carried out of the building, but now, she was regaining consciousness and trying to untangle herself from her garments, clearly confused and disoriented, but thankfully, alive.

Ms. Poole had no idea what she had stumbled upon, but she had no intention of abandoning these girls to whatever fate this group of men had in store for them. She had to do something, but whatever that something was, she couldn't do it alone. She turned to the streets of Berkeley for help and started trying to flag down cars. Several drivers refused to stop, ignoring her completely or swerving to avoid her. Most of the ones that did stop only paused long enough to tell her that they didn't want to get involved. Finally, she managed to convince a reluctant driver with a cell phone to call 911 and very soon, she heard the glorious sound of sirens in the distance. As the sirens grew louder, the Indian men released the crying girl and most of them seemed to simply vanish, nonchalantly ducking into storefronts and blending into the gathering crowd.

Police and firefighters arrived, and while they were securing the area, a third young Indian girl was found lying in a heap on the floor of the dark stairwell Ms. Poole had seen the men emerge from. The girl was unconscious and unresponsive to any attempts to rouse her. With one witness completely unconscious, one only barely awake and another in hysterics, the police had their work cut out for them in trying to get a handle on the strange situation.

As they attempted to question the hysterical girl, they found that she did not speak English, only Telugu, a language of southern India. Although Berkeley has a large South Asian population and there were many Indian people who had appeared at the scene, the police had trouble finding anyone who was willing to serve as an interpreter. That was when the imposing, round-faced man who had tried to intimidate Ms. Poole stepped forward and offered his services. He introduced himself as Lakireddy Bali Reddy, a name that was well known in the Bay Area.

Lakireddy Bali Reddy was a multimillionaire restaurateur and property mogul, and the living embodiment of the American dream. He had immigrated to the United States from India in 1960 to study chemical engineering at the University of California in Berkeley, but after earning his master's degree and working in that field for several years, he decided to go into business for himself. In 1975, he opened the Pasand Madras Indian Cuisine Restaurant on Shattuck Avenue in downtown Berkeley, just around the corner from where he now stood, talking to the police. The restaurant was a huge and almost immediate success, and while one prosperous business might have been enough for many men, Reddy was far too ambitious to stop there. He used the money he earned from his restaurant to buy cheap, dilapidated apartment buildings in the Berkeley area, then fix them up and rent them out. As his profits increased, so did his empire. He bought building after building until he owned apartments all across the East Bay. Over time, his company amassed more than one thousand apartment units that generated over one million dollars in rent every single month. He became the largest and richest landlord in the city; only his *alma mater*, the University of California, housed more Berkeley residents than he did. Reddy Reality was a Bay Area institution, and although his company was known for some shady practices, including poor maintenance and refusal to return tenants' security deposits, he made up for it with his generous philanthropy, both in Berkeley and in his home village in India. Reddy was worth over sixty million dollars and was viewed as a pillar of the community, and the police were more than happy to accept his help in sorting out the confusing situation.

Reddy explained to the police that the hysterical girl was eighteen-year-old Laxmi Patati and she was an employee at his restaurant. His realty company owned the apartment building where Laxmi lived with her two roommates, seventeen-year-old Sitha Vemireddy, the girl found in the stairwell, and Sitha's fifteen-year-old sister, Lalitha, the semi-conscious girl the men had thrown into the back of the van. According to Reddy, Laxmi said that she had been out running errands and had returned home to find Sitha and Lalitha lying unconscious in the apartment. Because of her extremely tenuous grasp on the English language, instead of calling an ambulance, she called Reddy's restaurant for help. Reddy said that he and his colleague, Venkateswara Vemireddy, Sitha and Lalitha's father, hurried over to the building right away and were in the process of rushing the girls to the hospital when Ms. Poole intervened.

An ambulance transported Sitha and Lalitha to Alta Bates Hospital where it was determined that the girls had suffered from carbon monoxide poisoning. Lalitha was treated and released the next day, but sadly, Sitha was pronounced dead on arrival. Even worse, an autopsy revealed that the teenage girl had been about ten days pregnant when she died. Keeping with Hindu tradition (even though the girls' parents were Christian), Reddy saw to the funeral arrangements himself and paid to have Sitha's remains cremated.

Investigators discovered that a blocked heating vent had caused the carbon monoxide fumes to leak into the girls' apartment. Reddy had recently had some work done on the roof and the debris the workers left behind had clogged the ventilation system. Further investigation revealed that there were a total of sixty-three leaks in the building, putting almost everyone who lived there in mortal danger. Although landlords are usually held accountable for negligence of such a grand scale, especially when it results in the death of a tenant, Berkeley police absolved Reddy of any guilt or responsibility, and thanked him for his helpful assistance in the matter.

Marcia Poole, however, did not believe Reddy's story. She hounded the police for days, claiming that Reddy had been involved in what she still believed was an attempted abduction and his translation of Laxmi's story should be considered suspect at best. But the Vemireddys didn't seem to agree with Ms. Poole. The girls' father claimed that he didn't blame Reddy for the death of his daughter at all. He blamed his own karma.

Ultimately, the authorities decided that the strange circumstances surrounding the ordeal that had occurred on Bancroft Way could be attributed to cultural differences that Americans simply couldn't understand. Sitha's death was ruled accidental, and the case was closed.

Chapter 2: The Berkeley Jacket

When classes resumed at Berkeley High School after the Thanksgiving holiday, the editing staff of the school newspaper got together to brainstorm about stories for the next edition of *The Berkeley Jacket*. Rick Ayers, the faculty advisor, brought up an article he had read in *The San Francisco Examiner* over the break about Sitha Vemireddy. It was a tragic tale of a young woman who had only arrived in the United States a few months ago and never got the chance to live out her shot at the American dream. The piece had been very moving and well written enough, but there was one question that occurred to Ayers that the reporter who wrote the article had neglected to answer or apparently even ask: why weren't Sitha and Lalitha Vemireddy in school?

The apartment where Sitha died was only a few blocks from Berkeley High School. By all rights, she and Lalitha should have been students there, and Ayers wanted to know why they weren't. He suggested to news editor Iliana Montauk that she have someone on the staff look into it and Iliana assigned the story to fifteen-year-old sophomore, Megan Greenwell.

Megan's initial research did little to clear things up. In fact, it only muddied the waters even more. She could find no good reason explaining why the Vemireddy sisters worked in a restaurant instead of to school or why they lived with an eighteen-year-old girl in a separate apartment—actually, an entirely separate building—from their parents. These were details that seemed to stand out to Megan as red flags and raised a number of obvious questions, but apparently, no one else was bothering to ask them. Apart from some well-meaning follow-up articles about the dangers of carbon monoxide poisoning and the need for detectors to be installed in rental properties, there was nothing more written about Sitha Vemireddy. In a matter of days, she would be completely forgotten. But as Megan pored over what little information she could find, she noticed that there was a name that seemed to be stamped in red ink across Sitha's life and death: Lakireddy Bali Reddy.

Reddy owned the Pasand restaurant where Laxmi Patati, Sitha, Lalitha and the Vemireddy sisters' father, Venkateswara, were employed. The building where the girls had been poisoned and the neighboring building where their parents lived in a studio apartment were both owned by Reddy Reality. Reddy had been there when Sitha died and he had served as the Laxmi's interpreter for the police. He had even taken care of Sitha's funeral arrangements. There seemed to be no part of Sitha's life in America that wasn't in some way connected to the local multimillionaire.

Megan brought what she had learned to Ayers and Iliana. Everyone agreed that there was more to uncover about Sitha Vemireddy's link to Reddy, but it would have to start with a deeper understanding of Indian culture. Ayers introduced them to Dharini Rasiah, a teacher at the high school who worked extensively with South Asian immigrants, especially the young women of the community. After hearing the details that Megan had unearthed, Rasiah explained that it was fairly common for young Indian women to work in the homes or businesses of the people who paid for their transportation into the U.S. Unfortunately, it was also fairly common for this arrangement to be taken advantage of and in some cases, it could even turn into what amounted to indentured servitude.

The idea that there could be a form of slavery existing in modern day Berkeley, arguably the most liberal and progressive city in the country, was more than a little shocking to Megan and Iliana. They needed to know more, so Rasiah arranged for them to speak with some female students from the South Asian community. Over the course of their interviews, they learned that while most of Berkeley may have thought fairly highly of Lakireddy Bali Reddy, the Indian community absolutely idolized him. He was a shining symbol of immigrant success in America, and he had used that success to do so much good back in India. He had donated generously to many noble causes and was believed to have saved hundreds of his people from lives of poverty by helping them get into the United States.

It sounded as if they were saying that Reddy might have been involved in illegally transporting immigrants to the U.S., which was a major story in itself, but it was what happened *after* they got into the country that Megan and Iliana were most interested in, and that was when their interview subjects stopped talking. As Megan and Iliana tried to pry information out of them, it became clear very quickly that in spite of the love and admiration the Indian girls claimed to have for Reddy, they were also terrified of him. A man with the money and power to give so much is also capable of using that money and power to take things away. Speaking out against him could be very dangerous. The girls were afraid for themselves and they were afraid for their families back home in India.

It took a great deal of coaxing, but with Rasiah's help, Megan and Iliana gained the trust of some of the girls. They promised to keep their identities anonymous and swore that nothing they said would ever be traced back to them. Eventually, the girls began to open up, and most of their stories were very similar.

It was widely known among the Indian-American community that Reddy paved the way for the immigration of many people, mostly young women and girls, from India to the U.S. where they worked in his restaurant, apartment buildings and other businesses, and were usually paid next to nothing. What little money they did make was sent back to their families overseas. Reddy kept them all on a very short leash. Most of the girls he "sponsored" were not allowed to go to school or even permitted to learn English. They relied on him for everything. They had nothing but what he gave them, nowhere to go for help and no way to ask for it even if they did.

Megan and Iliana couldn't help but express how unfair they thought the arrangement was, but the girls they spoke to defended it. The way they saw it, Reddy's actions were well within his rights. He had gotten the girls out of India and into America. He had put roofs over their heads and food in their bellies. They had a shot at a better life in the United States that would not have been possible without him. Whomever Reddy brought to the U.S. was obligated to do whatever he wanted in order to repay their debt. The two American girls, however, disagreed with that assessment and decided that they had no choice but to expose Reddy's activities.

Megan knew what she had to do next, and was very intimidated to do it, but she wasn't just playing at journalist anymore. Whether she had wanted it or not, she was a real reporter uncovering a real story, and that meant she had to present it from every angle. She had to talk to Reddy himself.

Megan gathered her courage and walked into the Pasand Madras Indian Cuisine restaurant, just around the corner from Sitha and Lalitha Vemireddy's apartment. She approached the host and asked to speak to Mr. Reddy for an article she was writing in her school newspaper about Indian culture. The host raised an eyebrow at her, then excused himself and went into the kitchen. A few moments later, he came back, looked Megan in the eye and said, "You need to leave right now."

Megan left.

The article that Megan and Iliana planned to write was a big story for such a little paper, and Ayers and the *Jacket* staff began to fear potential legal repercussions if and when it was published. Reddy was a powerful man in Berkeley and if he wanted to, he could sue the school, the faculty and the parents of everyone involved into oblivion. They consulted a lawyer (one of the parents of a *Jacket* staff member) who advised them on their potential liability, and then Megan and Iliana sat down and got to work. They focused on what they had learned about indentured servitude in the South Asian community and how a cultural class system could be taken advantage of and used to exploit lower-class Indian girls brought into America. They chose their words very carefully, acknowledging their lack of concrete evidence, but at the same time, implying Lakireddy Bali Reddy's involvement in the illegal and immoral practice.

The article was published on December 10th, 1999, two and a half weeks after Sitha Vemireddy's death. The newspaper staff and school faculty braced themselves, expecting a huge reaction from the community.

But there was no reaction. There was no reaction from Reddy, no reaction from the police, no reaction from the greater media and no reaction from the public. Days turned into weeks and the anticipation of the expected storm dwindled down to nothing. It seemed that the article wasn't the bombshell they thought it was, and by the time classes let out for winter break, it had been more or less forgotten.

No one had cared very much about Sitha Vemireddy's death, and apparently, no one cared about her life, either.

Or so it seemed.

Chapter 3: Slaves of Berkeley

Not long after the article ran in the *Jacket,* Berkeley
police received an anonymous letter claiming that Sitha
and Lalitha were not the daughters of Venkateswara
and Padma Vemireddy as Lakireddy Bali Reddy had told
them. There had actually been several anonymous tips
about Reddy throughout the month of December, some
of them referencing the article from *The Berkeley Jacket*
and accusing the magnate of importing illegal
immigrants from India. It seemed as if it were possible
that Marcia Poole, the woman who had first confronted
Reddy outside the Vemireddy girls' apartment, had been
right all this time. She had been harassing the police
ever since that day in late November, accusing them of
not investigating the circumstances surrounding Sitha's
death carefully enough. Police finally decided that at
least some of these allegations should be looked into, so
they put in a call to the Immigration and Naturalization
Service and asked them to re-interview Laxmi Patati,
Lalitha Vemireddy and Lalitha's supposed parents, but
this time bringing along their own interpreters.

When the INS first came knocking, Venkateswara Vemireddy stuck to his initial story, backing Reddy's claims as he had done before and blaming his own bad luck for his daughter's death. But then the questions turned to his background and the interviewers pointed out some odd discrepancies about the circumstances under which Vemireddy immigrated to the United States. According to his H1-B visa, he had come to America to work as a computer programmer at Active Tech Solutions, a Silicon Valley software company run by Reddy's son, Vijay Lakireddy. Instead, he was working at Reddy's Pasand restaurant for only a fraction of the salary he was supposed to be bringing in at Active Tech. Vemireddy claimed that his position at Vijay's company fell through, and he couldn't get a job as a computer programmer anywhere else. Reddy had then come to his aid, giving him employment at his restaurant and setting him up with two apartments where he and his family could live. But as the questions continued, holes started to emerge in his story, and it wasn't long before the roof caved in on him.

Vemireddy had no choice but to come clean. He admitted that he wasn't really the girls' father and in fact, Padma wasn't really his wife, either. She was his sister. He claimed that in India, Reddy had loaned him $6,500 and provided him with fraudulent visas and a phony job so he and his sister could get into the country. In return, they had to masquerade as husband and wife and escort Sitha and Lalitha out of India with them. Of course, Sitha and Lalitha weren't actually the girls' names, either. The deceased seventeen-year-old's real name was Chanti Prattipati.

Investigators moved on to the girls to get their stories. Laxmi Patati's version of events was likely the same as it had been on the day Chanti died, but when translated by someone other than Reddy, it came out very differently. What she said not only validated what *The Berkeley Jacket* had reported, but also revealed that as deep as Megan Greenwell and Iliana Montauk had dug, they had just scratched the surface of the story. Reddy's use of immigrants as indentured servants was only the tip of the iceberg.

Eighteen-year-old Laxmi said that she was also living in America under a false name and had been sold to Reddy by her father when she was only twelve years old. For years, she worked at Reddy's estate in India and served him whenever he was in the country. Now that Reddy had brought her to America, she continued serving him by working in his restaurant and rental properties...but the main reason she had been brought to the U.S. was to serve as Lakireddy Bali Reddy's personal sex slave. To the shock and disgust of the INS and the Berkeley police, Laxmi claimed that Reddy had been keeping her as a concubine for years, forcing her to have sex with him whenever he wanted. And she wasn't alone.

Laxmi said that she had accompanied Reddy to the airport on the day Padma Vemireddy arrived in San Francisco with Chanti Prattipati and her sister. He picked them up and drove them to the apartment he wanted the three girls to share and sent Padma next door to the neighboring building where she would live with her brother. When Reddy was alone with the three girls, he forced the fifteen- and seventeen-year-old sisters to have sex with him while Laxmi sat quietly and waited for him to finish. Over the next three months, until Chanti's death, Reddy had come to their apartment whenever the urge struck him, sometimes staying for days at a time. He even made sure he kept a bottle of Viagra in their medicine cabinet, just in case. Sometimes he wanted just one of the girls, sometimes all three. It didn't matter. Whatever he wanted, the girls believed they had no choice but to give it to him. It was possible that Chanti's unborn child that died with her was fathered by Reddy.

On January 18th, 2000, two days before he was going to leave the country for India, Lakireddy Bali Reddy was arrested and charged with "importing aliens for the purpose of prostitution and for other immoral purposes." A loud and angry public outcry soon followed. No one in the greater San Francisco area could believe that third-world horrors were occurring right under their noses. The fact that a prominent businessman and philanthropist was sexually abusing underage girls sparked heated outrage in the community. How had this gone unnoticed for so long, especially after the death of one of his concubines? The Berkeley police had no choice but to publicly apologize for their earlier lackluster investigation, with Lt. Cynthia Harris admitting it was a mistake to let Reddy serve as an interpreter on the day Chanti died, and that the error had delayed bringing him to justice.

In the weeks to come, it would be revealed that Reddy was the mastermind of a vast conspiracy, bringing underage girls into the country with the help of his family and friends while exploiting his cultural heritage by treating these girls any way he desired. His criminal activities probably began about fourteen years prior to Chanti's death, but the roots of his behavior and sense of entitlement dated back thousands of years. Although it's very doubtful that Reddy didn't at least question the morality of what he was doing, it is possible that he believed that his actions were completely justified.

He was, after all, a Reddy.

Chapter 4: Untouchables

India is a country of over one billion people, and 80% of them are Hindu. One-fifth of that 80%, somewhere between one hundred-fifty and two hundred million people, are dalits, or "untouchables," according to the Hindu caste system.

For thousands of years, this caste system operated as a form of apartheid and was enforced as law in India. Caste has nothing to do with the color of a person's skin or the region in which a person is born, but is a distinction that is assigned at birth, handed down from generation to generation, and it is virtually impossible to change. Caste dictates many things about a Hindu person's path in life, including whom he or she is allowed to marry and what his or her occupation will be. Those born into the highest caste are essentially considered royalty and are trained to become priests and scholars, the most revered people in the culture, while those born into the lowest caste have little choice but to become servants and manual laborers.

But a dalit is beneath even the lowest caste. When a person is branded a dalit, it means that he or she has no caste at all, which makes them to be considered by many as less than human. Some believe that if people with caste make the mistake of touching a dalit, they must undergo a purifying ritual to remove the contamination (hence the "untouchable" label). Traditionally, the only work dalits were allowed to do was jobs that had been rejected by people with caste. If a dalit could find any work at all, it was usually something along the lines of cleaning toilets and sewers or handling dead bodies. The name "dalits" literally translates into "broken people," and although Mohandas Gandhi rechristened them "Harijan" or "children of God," that term is now often used derogatorily and with sarcasm.

Following India's independence from Great Britain in 1947, caste-based discrimination was declared illegal by their constitution, but it would be very naïve to believe that just because a practice that had been in effect for millennia had been outlawed, that it suddenly ceased to exist. The Hindu culture is steeped in tradition and deep-rooted social conventions are difficult to change. Thanks in large part to an affirmative action program called "reservations," which saves spaces for dalits in schools and government positions, they have made enormous strides towards equality over the years, but only in India's biggest cities and most forward-thinking areas. To this day, there are places where dalits are still held down, where they are discriminated against and treated as subhuman, and by most accounts, Lakireddy Bali Reddy's home village of Velvadam in the southern state of Andhra Pradesh is one of those places. Although Velvadam lies in the Krishna district, one of the most affluent areas of Andhra Pradesh, Velvadam is a place of poverty and squalor. It is a village of eight thousand people, many of which are illiterate, most of whom are dalits.

Lakireddy Bali Reddy was born in Velvadam in 1937, and although the Reddys were far from wealthy, they were the richest family in the village. The region-wide Reddy caste is not the highest in Hindu culture, but to the dalits, they might as well be aristocracy. Throughout history, members of the Reddy caste were landowners and caretakers of small farming villages, and that was the case in Velvadam. The Reddys lorded over the village, owning much of the land and employing many of the village's inhabitants in their mango groves and rice fields. It was under the Hindu caste system that Reddy was raised, and what it taught him was that he was better and far more important than anyone else around him. From an early age, it was instilled in him that the purpose of almost everyone he knew was to serve him in any way he saw fit.

At the age of seventeen, Reddy married a thirteen-year-old girl, the first of three marriages, none of which would last very long. He then attended Osmania University in the city of Hyderabad, roughly an eight-hour drive west, where he earned two bachelor's degrees. In 1960, although it was extremely rare at the time, especially for citizens of rural villages, his family sent him abroad to earn his master's degree at the University of California in Berkeley, and it was there that Reddy made his second home.

Over the next quarter century, while he was amassing his vast restaurant and real estate fortune, Lakireddy Bali Reddy (or L.B. as he was becoming known as he assimilated into life in America) never forgot where he came from. Twice every year, he returned to Velvadam during the festivals of Mahashivrati and Vinayaka Chaturthi and threw lavish celebrations. Every time he came back, he was richer and more successful than the time before, and he made sure everyone knew it. His success seemed almost mythical to the people of his home village, who thought of America as a land of dreams, a faraway place full of luxuries and opportunities that they would never get the chance to experience for themselves. But Reddy was actually doing it, and every time he returned, they looked upon him with more and more awe and reverence.

Although the last half of the twentieth century saw great social, industrial and technological reform in India, secluded, rural villages like Velvadam were slow to reap those benefits. But Velvadam had something other villages like it didn't have—it had Lakireddy Bali Reddy. Over the years, he pumped millions of dollars into the village, building Velvadam into a more advanced, much more livable place. He built two elementary schools and a high school so his people could be educated. He created sources of clean drinking water so the villagers would no longer be forced to rely on ponds and streams contaminated by chemical runoff from nearby factories and power plants. He constructed a new wing at the local hospital to provide better medical care. He built five temples to Krishna so no one would ever have to go far to worship the favorite Hindu god of the region. He even opened a college in a neighboring township with his name on it: the Lakireddy Bali Reddy College of Engineering.

But the building up of Velvadam was not entirely for the villagers' benefit. His once modest ancestral estate was transformed into a massive and ostentatious compound. He had the lawns manicured to perfection and the gardens adorned with palm trees, tropical flowers and ornate statues of various Hindu gods. He left the small home he grew up in more or less as it had always been, but he built a three-story mansion behind it. The paradise he created in the center of the impoverished village was surrounded by a great wall to ensure that the villagers he loved and cared for stayed a respectful distance away from him. The grounds could only be accessed by an iron gate with the words: "L.B. Reddy Estates" written across the front. Though the extent of Reddy's philanthropy inspired Andhra Pradesh's Chief Minister Nara Chandrababu Naidu to bestow Velvadam with the nickname, "Little America," in truth, it was more of an accurate reflection of India as a whole—abject poverty butting right up against extreme wealth.

There is no doubt that Reddy did great things for his home village of Velvadam. It is indisputable that his money improved the quality of life for many of his people. But it is fair to question his motives. His extreme generosity was probably less about altruism than it was about transforming himself into a folk hero among his people. And indeed, he became more than just a hero. He became a god.

In 1986, Reddy made the decision to begin exploiting all the goodwill he had been cultivating with his philanthropy. At that time, he already owned many properties in Berkeley, and needed to staff them with cheap labor. And labor didn't come any cheaper than the dalits of Velvadam. They served him when he was visiting in India and if he could just get them into United States, he knew they would serve him there, too. The way he saw it, he would be doing them a favor. Everyone dreamed of a life in America. Everyone wanted a shot at the success that Reddy had achieved. He convinced them that with his help, they could have it...as long as they repaid their debts to him first. So with the assistance of his sons, Vijay and Prasad, and his younger brother Jayaprakash, Reddy started up an operation that provided a back door into America for the poor people of Andhra Pradesh.

The manufacture of phony passports and visas was a thriving business in most major Indian cities, including nearby Hyderabad, where Reddy had been educated and still had many influential contacts. He used his connections to enlist a team of agents whose jobs were to secure the documents he needed. If the police or other government officials caught wind of the illegal activity, Reddy used his significant wealth to bribe them into looking the other way. He often structured visas claiming that the holders would be working at Vijay's software company, but almost none of the people who used these visas were remotely qualified for technological work and all ended up working menial jobs in Reddy's businesses.

Once they landed in America, the illegal immigrants found that there was no feasible way to get out from under Reddy's thumb. The money they owed him for their transportation into the United States was a debt that was impossible to pay off under the terms that he dictated. In spite of the promise of a mutually beneficial arrangement, Reddy was the only person reaping any rewards. Without having to pay salaries and health benefits or even an hourly minimum wage, Reddy was able to amass an incredible fortune and become one of the wealthiest men in Berkeley with the help of a stable of people who were completely beholden to him. In Velvadam, he may have been the people's savior, but in Berkeley, he was their master.

It is unknown exactly how many people Reddy assisted in illegally immigrating into America between 1986 and 1999, but the number is thought to be somewhere in the neighborhood of five hundred. Half of them where young, underage girls like Chanti Prattipati.

Chapter 5: The Arrangement

Jarmani Prattipati was very poor, even by the standards of the dalits of Velvadam. He earned only one dollar a day, hauling water and concrete for construction crews, and every night, he would go home to his hut where he lived with his wife and five children in a segregated part of the village. They had no electricity and no running water and lived in a house with walls made of mud and a thatched roof made of stalks of bamboo. The only possession that his family had that was of any value at all was a milking buffalo that they kept tied up in the tiny patch of land they called their front yard.

Around 1996, Jarmani's oldest daughter had been married and while it was a joyous occasion in many ways, it had also left him even more financially destitute than he had been before. He had been forced to part with his life savings of one thousand dollars for the dowry, and although he still had three other daughters, there was no way he could afford to marry them all off. Dowries were out of the question, not to mention the wedding parties the family of the bride was expected to host. So when Lakireddy Bali Reddy paid him a visit and offered to take two of his daughters off his hands, Jarmani Prattipati saw him as his savior.

The Prattipati sisters were fairly typical targets of Reddy, and by the time he set his sights on them, he was well practiced in the art of extracting girls from their families. He went to Jarmani as a friend, offering him the chance to allow his daughters to work as maids in his Velvadam estate. That alone was a great opportunity, as it meant the girls would be fed and housed in the mansion, which would lift a huge financial burden from Prattipati's shoulders. But Reddy also promised that if he was satisfied with the work the girls performed, he would arrange for their transportation to the United States. Once the girls were in America the world would open up for them, just as it had for Reddy. There was no limit to what could be achieved in the U.S., even for a dalit, and it was possible that the girls could break Jarmani free from the poverty in which his lack of status had imprisoned him. It was a chance that wasn't offered to just anyone and it would have been foolish to refuse. So Jarmani Prattipati didn't just hand over with his twelve- and fourteen-year-old daughters to Lakireddy Bali Reddy, he did so gladly.

Whether Jarmani and his wife knew what Reddy really did with the girls behind the walls of his estate is uncertain. Reddy took young girls away from their families and into his bed so boldly and so often that it seems as if it would have been impossible for the people of Velvadam to not at least suspect what he was doing. But Reddy had spent years positioning himself as a god to the villagers. He had done so much good that it was difficult for them to accept that he was capable of such evil as well. But the sad truth is that if they knew the full extent of the abuse, their customs dictated that they could do nothing about it. And even if they had the courage to go against the traditions, the rest of the village would have turned against them, fearing that Reddy would retaliate by ceasing his philanthropic activities. So Jarmani Prattipati continued his life of hard labor while his daughters were condemned to service the sexual desires of a man old enough to be their grandfather. The girls remained in Reddy's mansion for three years, doing whatever Reddy required whenever he was in town.

When Reddy made his biannual trip to Velvadam in August of 1999, he distributed Viagra to many of the men throughout the village, singing its praises and promising that it would keep them young, like it did with him. It was that summer that he decided it was time to bring the Prattipati girls back with him and he began making the necessary arrangements.

By that time, Reddy had allegedly transported hundreds of people to America, and had it worked out to a science. It had become a very simple matter, so easy that maybe he had gotten a little lazy with it. He recruited Venkateswara and Padma Vemireddy to help him, set up the Prattipati sisters with their new identities, purchased all the counterfeit passports and visas he needed, then flew back to Berkeley and awaited the arrival of his two newest concubines.

During the three months the Prattipati girls spent in the United States, enduring Reddy's Viagra-assisted abuse on a regular basis, they sent the little money he paid them back to their parents in Velvadam. Their father used the meager earnings to upgrade his home from a mud-walled hut to a one-room concrete structure. His new shelter was the full measure of what he had gained from the sacrifice of his daughters.

Chapter 6: Outrage and Support

After his arrest in January of 2000, Reddy was released from incarceration on ten million dollars in bail and confined to his brother's mansion in Merced. There was some concern that he was a flight risk, even with such a high bond against him, so the judge constructed the bail to result in steep financial penalties against his family members if he fled. He used his limited freedom to give interviews to the press, often claiming that he was innocent of the charges against him and complaining that he was a man with many problems. All he had ever done was try to help people and look where it had gotten him. When questioned about whether he ever had sex with the young women he brought over from India, he declined to answer, although he did say that he thought they were all over eighteen.

As word of Reddy's crimes and the horrible extent of them spread throughout the community, a parent of a student at Berkeley High School called *The San Francisco Examiner* and informed them about the story that ran in *The Berkeley Jacket* a month earlier, which may have inspired the anonymous tips that ultimately led to Reddy's arrest. Reporter Matthew Yi contacted Megan Greenwell and Iliana Montauk for an interview and wrote an article about their investigation in which he credited the high school students as being the first to discover and expose the truth about Reddy. The fact that two teenage girls had uncovered a story about the exploitation of girls their own age was too good for the greater media to ignore. Even though professional journalists had to admit to having been outperformed in their jobs by high school students, it made for a great story, and Megan and Iliana were transformed into local celebrities. The Northern California Society of Professional Journalists even bestowed them with the "Journalist of the Year" award, making them the first non-professionals to ever receive the prestigious commendation.

At first, Megan and Iliana were honored by the attention they were receiving. They loved being quoted in newspapers and interviewed on TV and the radio, just as virtually every high school student would. But soon, they began shying away from the spotlight. They were afraid that the story was becoming about them instead of Chanti Prattipati and the many other young women who had been raped on a regular basis and had suffered in slavery for years while two communities separated by thousands of miles turned a blind eye to the glaringly obvious signs of abuse and exploitation.

But Chanti was not forgotten. In June of 2000, in a direct response to Reddy's crimes, Diana Russell and B.J. Miller founded the organization Women Against Sexual Slavery (WASS) to educate the public about the horrible indignities that Chanti and many other girls like her had suffered. The group arranged protests of the businesses of Lakireddy Bali Reddy, including a boycott of his Pasand restaurant.

While the city of Berkeley condemned Reddy and praised the people who had helped bring him to justice, his hometown of Velvadam had a decidedly different reaction. When American reporters traveled to the rural Indian village to get a deeper understanding of the story as it unfolded, they found a nearly unanimous outpouring of support for Reddy and his family. Villagers hung banners outside the windows of their tiny, dilapidated homes bearing slogans such as, "Lakireddy is our God. Leave him alone," and "Lakireddy is innocent." The man who had sexually abused the daughters of Velvadam was compared to Mother Teresa by its residents. The only people in the village who seemed to believe the allegations against him were the people whom Reddy had refused to help enter the United States.

By that time, Jarmani Prattipati was aware that one of his daughters had died, but he didn't know which one until a reporter for *The San Francisco Examiner* came into town to interview him and his wife. Weeks earlier, Jarmani had asked his relatives to ask one of Reddy's brothers, who was vacationing in Velvadam, the details about what had happened to his daughter. Reddy's brother replied that he was only in town for a holiday and was not interested in involving himself in the affairs of his brother. Besides, he didn't know the Prattipati family personally and had nothing to say to them. Why would he allow himself to be questioned by a family of dalits? Reddy's brother said little to the press, but he did state that Reddy's only mistake had been in helping so many people. His position was that when you're known for doing so much good, people try to take advantage of you, and when you cannot help some people, those people will try to destroy you.

Reddy's family members weren't the only ones making excuses for him, either. There was no shortage of explanations for the allegations among the people of Velvadam. Some thought the charges were invented because Americans could not stomach the idea of such a rich and successful Indian man in their country. The father of the girl who had become known as Laxmi Patati—the girl who had bravely told INS investigators about Reddy's ring of sexual slavery—even came to Reddy's defense. He told the reporters that he did not believe his own daughter's story and claimed there was no way that Reddy would have exploited the children of Velvadam. The Prattipati girls' mother had a similar reaction, stating that she did not believe the charges against Reddy, denied that she and her husband had sold their daughters to Reddy three years prior, and claimed that she didn't understand why her daughter would say such terrible things about a fine man such as Lakireddy Bali Reddy.

Even though it was well established that Reddy began sexually abusing underage girls in Velvadam, the Congress of Andhra Pradesh claimed that they could not charge Reddy for his alleged crimes because they had never received a single complaint about Reddy from anyone. Of course, even if any dalit villagers had dared to speak out against Reddy, it probably wouldn't have mattered. The president of the congress had a niece who was married to one of Reddy's sons.

Chapter 7: Trials and Sentences

Although authorities were able to get Reddy's young victims to talk to them and assist in the investigation, many of them refused to testify in court. Even in the new millennium, in the rural communities of India there was a still a stigma attached to crimes of a sexual nature. The victims of rape and statutory rape were (and in some cases still are) often seen to carry as much of the blame as those who committed the crimes against them. And there was not only shame involved, but there was also a high degree of fear that Reddy would use his power and influence to harm the girls and their families. And of course, there was still the ingrained cultural belief that because the victims were dalits, Reddy had the right to do whatever he wanted to them. It seemed as if no one involved in the crimes, neither the perpetrators nor the victims, understood just how horrible the sexual assault of minors is considered in the United States. Consequently, it made it very tough for the prosecution to build a substantial case against Reddy and his family, in spite of the fact that the investigation was being conducted by multiple agencies, including the INS, the FBI, the IRS, the Department of Labor and the Berkeley Police Department. The backwards mentality of almost everyone involved opened the door for plea-bargaining, and in the opinion of many, it also enabled Reddy to escape the full measure of justice.

In October of 2000, Reddy, his sons Vijay and Prasad, his brother Jayaprakash, and Jayaprakash's wife Annapurna, were all expected to enter guilty pleas as part of a "package deal" that included all five family members. However, the deal was to be made behind closed doors, which a media lawyer pointed out was illegal. Judge Saundra Brown Armstrong, who was assigned to the case, agreed with the media lawyer and opened the courtroom to the public. Admitting to sex crimes in a public forum was something Reddy was not prepared to do, so the defense asked for and was granted more time to prepare. Plea-bargaining and sentencing was postponed to the following year.

In the months that followed, Reddy's sons changed their minds about pleading guilty and instead decided to fight the charges against them. Also, while the case faced more delays, Jayashri Srikantiah, a lawyer for the American Civil Liberties Union Federation, filed a class action suit against the Reddys on behalf of the Prattipati family and the other victims.

On March 5th, 2001, almost a year and a half after the death of Chanti Prattipati, Jayaprakash and Annapurna Lakireddy arrived in Judge Armstrong's courtroom to enter their guilty pleas while Reddy's son Prasad, who had been very publicly proclaiming his innocence, sat with his lawyer in the audience bleachers behind them. When Judge Armstrong asked how Jayaprakash pleaded to the charges of manufacturing false documentation and importation of illegal aliens from India for sexual and labor exploitation, his admission of guilt was barely audible. Prasad leaned forward and put a hand on his uncle's shoulder as if to comfort him, but Jayaprakash turned and glared at him angrily until Prasad removed his hand and then awkwardly shuffled out of the courtroom. Annapurna was next, and she admitted her guilt while crying softly.

Lakireddy Bali Reddy, uncharacteristically dressed in sneakers and a rumpled suit, also appeared in court that day. He was initially supposed to enter his plea along with his brother and sister-in-law, but because he would be pleading guilty to a violent crime, it meant that he would have to be placed in jail while he awaited sentencing. Both the prosecution and the defense were lobbying the court to let Reddy remain free so that it would be easier for him to liquidate his assets and pay the two million dollars in restitution that he had agreed to give to his victims. Judge Armstrong ordered all the attorneys to submit their arguments in briefs citing legal reasons why Reddy should be allowed to await sentencing outside of jail, and reconvene in two days. In the meantime, Reddy signed documents asserting his intention to plead guilty. Afterwards, the ACLU and prosecuting attorneys expressed that they were content, stating to the press that these pleas were only the beginning.

On March 7th, Reddy returned to the Oakland courtroom to officially enter his guilty plea. Judge Armstrong rejected the lawyers' requests to allow Reddy to remain out on bail, stating that they had not presented a compelling reason why the law should not apply in this case. She ordered that after his plea, Reddy would be taken into custody. Judge Armstrong then read Reddy his rights and listed the charges against him: one count of conspiracy to bring illegal immigrants into the United States, two counts of transporting minors for the purpose of sex and other immoral purposes, and one count of tax evasion. In exchange for pleading guilty to those charges, the Assistant U.S. Prosecuting Attorney John Kennedy agreed that he would not charge Reddy with the far more serious crimes of rape and statutory rape. In addition, Reddy would not be called as a witness to testify in the trials of his sons, who were both still planning to plead not guilty. And finally, although he faced a potential sentence of thirty-eight years, Kennedy recommended and Judge Armstrong agreed that Reddy should spend between five and six years in prison, as well as pay two million dollars in restitution to the Prattipati family, the young woman who had become known as Laxmi Patati and another unnamed victim who suffered similar abuse. The unnamed victim was eleven years old.

After stating that he understood the charges against him and entering his guilty plea, Reddy addressed the court in tears, saying, "I want to apologize to you, to the court, to my family. I am very, very sorry. Please excuse me." His son, Vijay, wept at Reddy's words, and so did Nalini Shekar, a Telugu interpreter and counselor who had been working with Reddy's teenage victims over the past year. But while Vijay wept in sorrow, Shekar's tears were tears of joy. Reddy waved goodbye to his son and was escorted out of the courtroom by two U.S. Marshals.

Although the day in court was considered to be a victory by some, it wasn't nearly enough for many people who were close to the case. Diana Russell and her organization, Women Against Sexual Slavery, began a letter-writing campaign, angry that the sentence that Reddy would likely be handed did not fit the scope of his crimes. Five or six years in prison and two million dollars in restitution seemed like little more than a slap on the wrist for a criminal enterprise that spanned fourteen years and took advantage of hundreds of victims, many of them children, many of whom had been raped.

In response to the public outcry, Reddy's attorney, Ted Cassman, pointed out Reddy's philanthropy in Berkeley and in Velvadam, suggesting that he had already—preemptively—made financial amends for his crimes. He also pointed out Reddy's first marriage when he was seventeen to a thirteen-year-old girl and argued that Reddy comes from a culture where intimacy with young girls is accepted. Backlash against that statement was strong and swift. The idea that rape and sexual slavery should be accepted as cultural differences was rejected across the board, but especially by the Indo-American community. They felt as though the South Asian immigrant population's image had been tarnished enough by the despicable nature of Reddy's crimes. Trying to say that the people of their culture accepted the rape of young women was akin to saying that slavery should still be tolerated in the U.S. because it had happened in the past. Cassman's ill-conceived argument had backfired, and could have been disastrous for his client.

On June 19th, 2001, Reddy returned to court for sentencing, and it seemed that Russell's letter-writing campaign and Cassman's moronic statement had indeed had an effect. Judge Armstrong told the packed courtroom that she had changed her mind about accepting Reddy's plea. Due to the fact that the victims' psychological distress had not previously been taken into account, she had decided that Reddy deserved a longer sentence than the five-to-six-year term that had been agreed to. In the time that had passed since Reddy had entered his plea, the seven victims involved in the case had shown signs of severe psychological distress. One of them even regressed into childhood whenever she spoke of the abuse she had endured at Reddy's hands. These girls would need years of therapy and because most or all of them were not legal citizens, they would probably never get the care they needed.

Additionally, American investigators had discovered that Reddy loyalists were pressuring the victims and their families to not cooperate with the authorities, offering them bribes, and when that didn't work, threatening them. In April of 2000, shortly after Reddy entered his plea, Sivareddy Seelam, a former Berkeley resident, associate of Reddy's and potential witness in the case against him, was doused with acid outside his home in Velvadam. He survived, but his grandson died in the attack. The incident was never traced back to Reddy, probably because it was never thoroughly investigated by Indian authorities. Judge Armstrong, however, felt there was enough evidence to pursue a charge of obstruction of justice against Reddy and that would carry more fines and prison time with it.

After listing all of her concerns, the judge ordered the attorneys to leave the courtroom, work out another sentence and come back that afternoon. None of the attorneys, including ACLU attorney Jayashri Srikantiah, wanted to do this. Srikantiah claimed that the victims were happy with the six-year sentence and did not want to face the possibility of going to trial and forcing the girls to testify. Judge Armstrong said that while a trial might be hard on the witnesses, it could also be therapeutic.

After lunch, the attorneys came back with their adjustments. Instead of five or six years, they recommended an eight-year sentence. Apparently, considering the thirty-eight year maximum, the relatively small addition was enough to satisfy Armstrong, in spite of her tough talk that morning. She agreed to the sentence and even granted Reddy's request to serve his time in Lompoc Prison, a cushy institution for wealthy, white-collar criminals, popularly known as "Club Fed."

After Reddy's sentencing, it was time to clean up the scraps, although considering how lightly he had been treated, it was doubtful that the sentences of his co-conspirators would be very remarkable. Jayaprakash and Annapurna Lakireddy were scheduled to be sentenced on July 24th, 2001, and it was expected that Jayaprakash would receive a sixteen-month sentence and Annapurna one year, but Judge Armstrong postponed their sentencing until November 6th.

In October of 2001, Vijay Lakireddy's attorney, George Cotsirilos, tried to discredit the victims' testimony under the claim that the Telugu interpreters were biased. One of the interpreters, Baharat Koner, president of the Telugu Society, was known to have written a letter to Judge Armstrong, asking her to be harsh on the Reddy family. He had also participated in a demonstration outside the Pasand Restaurant hosted by Women Against Sexual Slavery. Nalini Shekhar, the counselor who had worked with the victims and wept tears of joy when Reddy plead guilty to his crimes, was also at the same demonstration. Judge Armstrong ruled the charges proved nothing. Any decent human being would side with Reddy's victims over Reddy himself and the fact that the interpreters found Reddy's actions deplorable didn't prove that they had done anything wrong.

But Cotsirilos's most serious charges were against a translator named Uma Rao. He claimed that Rao encouraged the victims to exaggerate their claims against Reddy and his family and even lie if necessary. Lending credibility to Cotsirilos's charges, on October 16th, Assistant U.S. Attorney Stephen Corrigan (who had taken over the case for the prosecution because John Kennedy had been promoted to a judgeship) acknowledged that four of the victims were in fact encouraged to embellish facts by Ms. Rao. Two of the victims also admitted that they had lied, although it is possible that all these confessions and changes of stories could have been in response to intimidation from Reddy and his supporters. Even so, these developments carried potentially devastating consequences towards the sentencing of the rest of the family and even threatened to overturn the light sentence that had been handed down to Reddy.

In response to the controversy, Reddy's brother and his wife considered withdrawing their guilty peas, but decided against it on the condition that Corrigan strike two statements from the pre-sentencing report. First, they needed it removed from the record that after they had been arrested, they had tried to arrange for some of the victims to be deported to India, and second, they wanted it struck that one of the victims had reported that Jayaprakash had sex with two of Reddy's victims. An agreement was made, but Judge Armstrong once again postponed the sentencing, this time to January 29th, 2002 and the charges were plea-bargained down to one count of immigration fraud each.

On December 12th, 2001, Judge Armstrong recused herself from the still unsettled Reddy cases, claiming a conflict of interests. Judge Claudia Wilken took her place, which resulted in still more delays in the proceedings. Finally, on April 29th, 2002, Judge Wilkin sentenced Jayaprakash Lakireddy to one year in a halfway house. He was allowed to stay out of prison so he could continue running his businesses. His wife, Annapurna, was sentenced to six months of electronically monitored home detention so she could care for her three children. She was allowed to go grocery shopping, attend religious events, doctor appointments and her kids' sports and school activities.

Vijay and Prasad Lakireddy were the only ones left, and both of them faced charges of immigration fraud and importing Indian girls for immoral purposes, including rape and sex with a minor. Like their father, they were also accused of traveling abroad to seek out girls for sexual activities, harboring, transporting and employing illegal immigrants over a fourteen-year period beginning in October of 1986. Prasad was also charged with attempting to intimidate a witness. Both still maintained their innocence, and Judge Wilken set their trial date for January 6th, 2003, but on April 29th, 2002, Vijay told the judge that he was willing to discuss a plea bargain.

Vijay admitted to falsifying a visa for Venkateswara Vemireddy, and in exchange, the other charges against him were dropped. He was scheduled to be sentenced in late September of 2002, but another unexplained delay pushed it to November. In the end, he was sentenced to two years in a minimum-security prison and forced to pay a $40,000 fine.

In March of 2004, Attorney Michael Rubin settled a civil suit against Reddy, winning $8.9 million for Chanti Prattipati's family, which was the closest thing to justice that came out of the years of investigations and trials.

Prasad Lakireddy's legal battle continued until June of 2004. Over the course of plea bargains and writs of *habeas corpus* to have his own pleas overturned, he ended up getting five years probation, one year of house arrest and a $20,000 fine.

Chapter 8: Aftermath

On April 2nd, 2008, Lakireddy Bali Reddy was released from prison. There was no media coverage, and afterwards, he quietly took up residence in a brand new mansion that he had built in the Berkeley hills while he served out his prison time. He is currently registered as a sex offender on the State of California, and still visits Velvadam twice a year, where he continues to enjoy the admiration of his people.

Although it's certainly arguable that Reddy and his family did not have to face the full force of justice for their horrible crimes, there is some good that came out of the whole ordeal. Largely because of a dialogue started by the Reddy case, Assembly Bill 22 was passed in 2005, California's first law setting high criminal penalties for human trafficking. The law imposed longer sentences, higher monetary restitutions and allowed for victims to bring civil action against their traffickers, even though they were not U.S. citizens.

It is also important to remember the heroes of the story, all of which, appropriately, are women. Without the bravery of Marcia Poole, Chanti Prattipati's death might never have been noticed by anyone. Without the tenacity of teenagers Megan Greenwell and Iliana Montauk, Reddy's ring of slavery might never have been exposed. And without the courage of Reddy's many victims who spoke out against him, he might never have faced any punishment at all. These women were instrumental in shutting Reddy's enterprise down and potentially saved hundreds of young girls from being subjected to rape and slavery.

Before the Lakireddy Bali Reddy scandal, there was little to no awareness regarding human trafficking and sexual slavery. It was an issue that was so foreign in concept, so outrageous and inhumane that few Americans could even wrap their minds around it. It seemed like something that could never have happened in the U.S., much less a place like Berkeley. But now, Lakireddy Bali Reddy is the poster boy for one of the most despicable crimes a person can perpetrate, and for years to come his name will be used to point out the extreme, sickening depths to which a human being is capable of sinking. But although his name is irreparably tarnished, Reddy will likely live out the rest of his days in the comfort and wealth he built on the backs of the hundreds of people he exploited.

References

http://www.wassusa.com/

http://sfpublicpress.org/news/2012-02/how-an-infamous-berkeley-human-trafficking-case-fueled-reform

http://www.berkeleyside.com/2009/12/08/ten-years-later-how-two-berkeley-high-reporters-broke-sex-ring-scandal/

http://www.bhsjacket.com/features/ten_year_anniversary_celebrated_jacket_story

http://articles.latimes.com/2001/nov/25/magazine/tm-7947

http://www.lbrce.ac.in/chairman.html

http://www.colosseumbuilders.com/Guild/h1b/library/Reddy/sfe20000207reddy.htm

http://en.wikipedia.org/wiki/Reddy

http://www.berkeleydailyplanet.com/issue/2004-06-08/article/19030?status=301

http://www.rediff.com/us/reddy.htm

http://en.wikipedia.org/wiki/Dalit

http://www.rediff.com/news/2000/feb/08lak.htm

http://ask.yahoo.com/20020722.html

http://speedydeletion.wikia.com/wiki/Lakireddy_Bali_Reddy

http://www.programmersguild.org/archives/lib/Reddy/sjm20000121reddy.htm

http://www.law.msu.edu/king/2003/2003_Harrison.pdf

http://www.dianarussell.com/why_did_chanti_die.html

http://www.berkeleydailyplanet.com/issue/2002-09-30/article/14972?headline=Sentencing-delayed-in-Lakireddy-case--Matthew-Artz

http://archive.dailycal.org/article/10295/sentence_handed_down_for_son_s_part_in_reddy_intri

The Forgotten Pirate Hunter

The True Account of American Librarian Ted Schweitzer Pursuit to Free Refuge At the End of Vietnam

By Reagan Martin

Prologue

November 16, 1979 was a beautiful day for flying. The weather was balmy, not a cloud in the sky, and visibility was clear for miles. As the helicopter roared over the turquoise blue ocean, the pilot kept his eyes peeled for any trouble, or damage, around the area he was required to check. The huge gas rigs, which soared above the water like skeletal fingers pointing to the sky, appeared to be in good shape and working fine. The pilot smiled, grateful for the sight. Not only would he be home early, but he knew his boss at the gas company where he worked would be pleased there were no problems to report.

Arcing the helicopter to the right, the pilot radioed in that all was secure, and then swung wide over the gulf of Siam to begin his return journey home. Passing above the tiny island of Koh Kra, an uninhabited atoll of rock and jungle approximately 34 miles from the shore of Thailand, he peered down, and then did a double take. The island was supposed to be uninhabited, but what he saw made him swing the chopper around again and do a second pass.

There below him, looking like tiny scraps of colored paper, were dozens, maybe hundreds of people, and no ships in sight. He knew the people shouldn't be there, yet he was not all that surprised to see them. He was well aware that Thai fishermen used the island as a prison to hold Vietnamese refugees, and undoubtedly this was a large group of them.

Perhaps 'fishermen' was too kind a word to describe those who literally kidnapped the Vietnamese boat people trying to escape their country. Pirates was much more appropriate.

Swinging the chopper back around, the pilot headed for home. He needed to alert someone, but he knew calling the Thai authorities, or any government officials, would be useless. They seemed oblivious to the plight of the Vietnamese refugees, and unconcerned about what happened to them. No, the pilot thought, he would call neither of those agencies. Instead, he would call the UNHCR (United Nations High Commission for Refugees).

Speaking to someone on the phone, the pilot described what he had seen. The man on the other end of the line asked if he would fly him back out to the island, but the pilot was reluctant. He didn't want to get involved. After some pleading however, he finally agreed.

Two days later the chopper was flying back towards Koh Kra Island, the official from UNHCR sitting next to him, binoculars on his lap and a tense, determined look on his face. Reaching the atoll, the official raised his binoculars and was appalled by what he saw. The people were still there, clearly visible, but now ships were there as well; pirate ships. As far as the man could tell, at least 20 of them rested just offshore. Scanning the island more widely, the official saw something that made his stomach turn. Bobbing in the surf, floating less than a hundred yards from shore, were numerous dead bodies.

"They're slaughtering them down there!" The official shouted. "We need to land!"

But the pilot, who had also noticed the bodies drifting in the sea, shook his head.

"I'm not hired to fly combat missions." He said, swinging the chopper around and beginning to gain altitude.

The man sitting next to him felt defeated and distressed, but he couldn't blame the pilot. He knew this was not the end. He would have to come back; he'd just have to find another way to get here.

Chapter One

Theodore Schweitzer, the official who sat next to the pilot in the helicopter flying over Koh Kra Island, was a man fiercely dedicated to issues he found morally inappropriate.

In the 1970's he had taken a job as a librarian at the international school in Bangkok, Thailand, and immediately fell in love with the land of Southeast Asia. He was fluent in both Thai, and French, and had married a stunning, dark haired Thai girl.

When his school contract ended, he had no desire to return the states and so took a position as a 'media consultant' at the American Air Force Base in Udorn, northeast Thailand. His job was for the defense department at the Ramasun Station, where he oversaw the highly sensitive secret archives.

While there, he was sent to Cambodia, just before the capital fell to the Khmer Rouge, where his assignment was to help salvage documents and equipment from the American military mission during the Vietnam War. It was during this time that Schweitzer realized he was in his element doing this type of work. He functioned well under pressure, and confusing situations only made his adrenaline pump faster. He quickly became skilled at using computerized systems, long before the 'world wide web' became a household word.

Between these skills, and his fluency in the Thai language, it was no surprise that in 1979 he was hired by the UNHCR as a field officer at the regional office in Bangkok. But Schweitzer was not one to sit behind a desk, and having seen the plight of the Vietnamese people while in Cambodia, he begged to be given a position in the 'field'.

"I'm a field officer." He told his boss at UNHCR. "I don't want to shuffle paper, I want to help refugees. Send me to the field."

Granting his wishes, the UNHCR assigned him to the port in Songkla, Thailand, where he lived in a comfortable house along the shore. But any relationship Schweitzer may have forged with Thai officials quickly deteriorated after he was approached by a woman who showed him a letter she had received from her Vietnamese daughter. The woman had not known what had become of the girl until the teen had somehow smuggled the letter to her mother, revealing that she, along with 16 other refugees, were being held in a brothel in Songkla.

Schweitzer went in and rescued the 17 Vietnamese girls, who had been kidnapped and forced into prostitution, and in doing so had brought upon himself the wrath of Thai police. The brothel, it soon became known, was owned in part by a Thai police officer.

Schweitzer had only been working for the UNHCR for a short time when the pilot of the helicopter called him about the mass of people spotted on Koh Kra Island. When the pilot refused to land, and they returned from their trip, Schweitzer immediately secured a Thai Marine Police patrol to sail him back to Koh Kra.

Reaching the shores of the little island, which was barely three and a half miles square, was difficult. Surrounded by a reef of white coral, which made beaching any watercraft virtually impossible, the boat would need to anchor off shore and use motorized rubber rafts and dinghy's, to reach land.

The pirate ships had since departed, and once Schweitzer and the men came ashore, they found 157 Vietnamese refugees, many hysterical, and in need of medical attention. Schweitzer did what he could to get the group stable, and then the men began the arduous task of bringing them back to the mainland.

Schweitzer would take the survivors to a refugee camp in Songkla, which was originally built in 1976 to house the inpouring of refugees entering the country. At that time the camp was small, and quickly ran out of room. So in 1978 construction for a bigger camp was begun, and was still a work in progress now. But by 1980 Songkhla Camp would contain 32 wooden barracks and house 6,000 refugees.

The camp was a lot like a prison, surrounded by a barbed wire fence, and patrolled daily by a company provided from the Thai army. It may not have seemed like the most accommodating of conditions, but compared to the fate of those refugees who fell into the hands of pirates, it could have been the Beverly Hills Hilton.

There were three wells on the property to provide fresh water for drinking and cooking, but no place to gather wood for the fires. UNHCR provided a monthly limit of charcoal, but it never seemed to be enough, and the refugees were forced to try and find other fuel to cook their food.

This, of course, aroused the greed in others to quickly rear its ugly head. The men who patrolled the camp encouraged their friends to open small markets outside the enclosure, and sell firewood and other goods for astronomical prices. Most of the refugees had no money, nor anyone on the outside to help them with income. For these people, charity would be their only means of survival.

Still, it was better than what happened to those who fell prey to the pirates, as Ted Schweitzer was learning, while listening to those he had just rescued from Koh Kra Island. The story they would tell was so horrific and brutal that it would stay with him for the rest of his life.

# # #

In a shaking voice, Nhat Tien, and the other refugees among the 157 just rescued revealed for Ted Schweitzer what had happened to them on their perilous journey from Vietnam to the desolate island of Koh Kra.

Pirates had attacked their boat just offshore, and had thrown most of them overboard into the sea. Those who could manage swam to shore, but seventeen of them couldn't make it and drowned trying.

When dawn broke those survivors huddled on the beach were met by the other Vietnamese who were already on the island. These fellow refugees told them that often pirates would tow entire boatloads of refugees to Koh Kra, where they would systematically rob them of any valuables and rape their women.

Nhat Tien and the others, although having heard horrific tales of what pirates did to the boat people from their country, were confused. The pirates who had attacked their boat had not followed them onto the island. But this fact alone was not enough for them to let their guard down. They would just have to wait and see what happened.

As the days passed and no pirates showed up, Nhat Tien and the others waited for help. They had virtually no food, very little water, and no means to leave the island, as their boat had been lost after the attack. Their hope was dwindling fast, and they prayed daily that a ship would come to rescue them. After a few days, a ship did stop by. But it was a ship loaded with pirates, and all too soon the refugees realized the only rescue they might offer was death.

As the pirates came ashore, they surveyed the women, grabbing any that caught their fancy, and throwing them to the ground. Then, stripping off her clothes, they would brutally rape her right in front of her husband, children, parents and all the others. The pirates took turns, each man having sex with as many women as he wanted, as the girls cried and pleaded for help. One girl would tell Schweitzer that she was raped 'hundreds' of times in little more than a 24-hour period.

Many of the refugee men, sickened by the sight of their women being brutalized, tried to intervene and were clubbed and beaten for their effort. One man, however, refused to be intimidated, and he bravely demanded that the pirates leave the women alone.

At first, the pirates were amused, laughing at the man and shoving him out of the way. But after a while, tired of the game, one of the pirates took an ax from his belt and swung it at the man, hitting him across the face. The refugee went down, and a second blow to the back of his head opened a wound several inches wide that sprayed blood and brain matter in a wide arc.

Those refugees who watched the murder began to scream in terror, but the pirates only laughed and continued to ravish the girls. They seemed oblivious to the dead man lying there, and the others who pleaded for mercy.

Every day, more pirate ships arrived, bringing different men to rape and ravish the women. Schweitzer would later learn that when women prisoners were on Koh Kra, word spread quickly among the pirates in the region, and hundreds of them would rush to the island to sample the new merchandise. Incredibly, on one single day, 50 ships had arrived to brutalize the girls, some of whom were literally raped to death.

On another day, the pirates lined up the refugees and examined each of their mouths. Taking one from the line, five pirates forced the man to the ground and held him down. Then, using a knife, one of them cut and pried the gold-filled teeth from the refugee's mouth.

After the first series of rapes, many of the women had scattered about the island, trying to find shrubbery and caves to hide in. Pirates would search, finding many, but at other times, they would simply torture the male refugees until they told them where they were hiding, or until the man's pitiful screams brought the women out on their own.

Schweitzer himself had come upon one of these hidden girls while he was on the island, and when he found her, her condition reduced him to tears.

The girl was young, barely in her teens, and for the past eighteen days she had been hiding in a rocky sea cave, trying to avoid the pirates. But the cave had not been a kind sanctuary for her. She had been forced to stand in waist deep water, and when Schweitzer finally pulled her from the cave, the girl could no longer walk. Her legs were little more than exposed bone, having been feasted on by sea crabs, and the caustic salt water had done the rest. The poor girls flesh was virtually rotted away.

Schweitzer was shocked and appalled by what he was hearing, although he later wondered why. He had seen the lighthouse himself, but until now, the words on it had not hit home.

On Koh Kra, there was an abandoned lighthouse that sat atop a concrete base. On the base were written these words:

KO KRA ISLAND – ISLAND OF THE DEVIL

The women and girls must hide

You must not let the Thai pirates see them

If they do they will be raped

The sign was only of help to refugees washed ashore or shipwrecked nearby. But for those brought to the island by pirates it did little good. There was simply no chance for anyone to hide at those times.

To Ted Schweitzer, Koh Kra appeared to be little more than a personal playground for area pirates. With anger mounting and his heart breaking, Schweitzer knew he would have to do anything in his power to help these people. And it didn't matter how many missions to the island it took.

Chapter Two

The troubles for the Vietnamese boat people began at the end of the Vietnam War, following the fall of Saigon. At that time, the Vietnam Socialist Government had very little sympathy for those citizens residing in such places as Cambodia, Laos, and especially South Vietnam. Those people had not only supported the foreign forces who had ravished their country, but in many instances, they had also fought against their own people of North Vietnam. This was an action the new government found unforgivable.

Rounding up these 'traitors', the Vietnamese Government sent hundreds of thousands of them to 're-education camps', which were little more than prisons. Here, without ever being tried, people were held, tortured, abused and very often killed. From South Vietnam alone, more than one million people were imprisoned in the camps.

By 1979, Vietnam was once again at war, this time with the People's Republic of China. The government ordered all of Vietnam's ethnic Chinese to either perform labor, or be imprisoned in a camp, an action that immediately set off an exodus of refugees fleeing the country.

The majority of the Chinese lived in the south, and had no way to escape Vietnam other than by boat. But it was a risky endeavor, evidenced by the UNHCR's estimation that between 200,000 and 400,000 of these refugees died at sea trying to escape. Many other groups put the figure even higher than that.

Those with money could either bribe high officials to help them leave, or secure passage on a large, seaworthy vessel. For most though, their only means of escape were in rickety, small wooden boats (and sometimes even rafts) that would be overcrowded, and forced to leave in the dead of night to avoid capture and imprisonment.

But once on the open water, the Vietnamese faced even greater hardships, being subjected to deadly storms, high seas, the risk of capsizing, disease, starvation, and of course, pirates.

The refugees were easy prey for the pirates because once they left Vietnam they lost the protection of the Vietnamese government. Worse yet, until they landed somewhere they were protected by no country at all. They were like lost souls blowing in the wind, with no home, no country, and no one at all to protect them.

There were other reasons the pirates targeted them as well. Because they could not take possessions in the small boats they traveled in, it was common practice for the refugees to sell everything they owned and convert the cash into easily transported gold. Since most pirates were poor Thai fishermen, robbing these pitiful souls was a quick and easy way to make money. And these men stole anything that could bring them a buck. Often, they would even steal the motors from these tiny boats, leaving the refugees to drift aimlessly in the ocean, dying a horrific death from thirst and starvation.

But it wasn't only stealing that brought the pirates wealth. There were the women too. Not only were the girls used for their own personal pleasure, but many pirates would kidnap these women and force them into prostitution on the mainland. Some, not wanting to go to the trouble and risk of bringing them back to port, would simply prostitute them from pirate ship to pirate ship, passing them around until they were literally raped to death, at which point they would be thrown overboard like little more than trash.

As savage as it may sound, to the Thai pirates the Vietnamese were getting what they deserved. To come across a boat full of virgin women was like karma to them, and they took what they felt they rightfully deserved. Perhaps they never realized that to a Vietnamese woman, being raped was one of the worst disgraces she could face.

Virginity is a prized possession to both Vietnamese women and men. For a woman to lose it, even through no fault of her own, is to suffer deep humiliation and rejection from a Vietnamese man. It is viewed as a dishonor and a disgrace, and as a result, many women do not report it.

The pirates knew there was no one to safeguard the Vietnamese boat people, and so they had little to fear from exploiting them. As a result, millions of these refugees were robbed, tortured, and abused by pirates in the South China Sea, while hundreds of thousands of them were murdered by them. But for others, it was still worse. And none of them would ever receive justice for what they endured.

#   #   #

After getting a firsthand look at the situation, Schweitzer knew that there was a lot of work to be done. He had no idea how deep the problem would run, or how difficult it would be to repress it. But he could not imagine anyone who wouldn't be sympathetic to the plight of the Vietnamese boat people. Unfortunately, he would find out that he was very wrong in that assumption.

Chapter Three

When Ted Schweitzer approached the Thai government to discuss the dilemma of the refugees and pirates, he was not surprised to find that they were not receptive to him at all. While not all the pirates were Thai citizens, the vast majority of them were, a fact that the Thai government refused to admit for several reasons.

First of all, the government was not anxious to receive the millions of refugees flooding their country. Their own citizens, the so-called pirates, were poor and struggling themselves. The Thai government was sympathetic and protective of their plight too, and they had no wish to fault them for what they needed to do to survive.

Schweitzer was also well aware of the animosity Thai officials felt towards a foreign agency attempting to enforce a criminal charge against one of their citizens. The Thai government's attitude bordered on hostility, and their demeanor towards Schweitzer was one of 'you're on your own.' For these reasons, among others, the Thai government stalled at taking any action against what was going on in the South China Sea. But that did not stop Schweitzer.

#   #   #

The next set of Vietnamese boat people Schweitzer would be credited with rescuing left Rach Gia, Vietnam on December 1, 1979. In a small wooden boat, carrying 107 refugees, the frightened group set sail for Thailand in the dead of night.

Three days into their journey, they encountered a pirate ship that sailed up next to them and forced them to stop. The pirates, realizing that the little boat was so overcrowded they couldn't even climb aboard, then ordered 27 of the Vietnamese onto their own ship. While those pirates who remained onboard surveyed the girls in the group, others moved onto the small wooden craft and plundered it, taking anything of value they found from the vessel, as well as from those still aboard.

Calling for a towline, the pirates then attached it to the small boat to their ship, and with 80 refugees still on board, began to sail away. If any of the Vietnamese believed they were being towed someplace, they were sadly mistaken. Instead, the pirate ship increased its speed, moving in a tight circle, until the little boat was whipping around behind it at an alarming rate of speed.

As the small boat began to spin faster and faster, water poured over the side, swamping the vessel and eventually sinking it. The 80 people left to struggle in the ocean were quickly abandoned, and left to drown. For some of the 27 now being held prisoner by the pirates, those who were now dying in the ocean would come to be viewed as the lucky ones.

The pirates sailed their captives to Koh Kra Island, but as they approached the little atoll, they apparently realized there were men among the 27 they carried. They had no need for males on the island, and so threw these men overboard, forcing them to try to swim ashore. For seven of them, it was an impossible task, and they perished in the choppy surf, several hundred yards from land.

Once on shore, the pirates subjected the refugees to intense questioning, torture, and repeated rapes. Each day gangs of pirates would arrive to subject them to the same treatment. Many of the women would try to hide in the jungle, but most were unable to elude their captors.

There was, however, one woman who was determined to avoid the pirates at all costs. She hid in the dense bushes and managed to evade the pirates for almost a week. Frustrated, or perhaps just lazy and evil, the pirates decided to light the jungle on fire to flush her out.

Terrified, and with her flesh burning, the woman ran from the inferno that threatened to overtake her. Arriving on the beach, her back blistered and peeling, the pirates subjected her to one of the most vicious rapes the others had ever seen. Screaming, and in agony, the girl pleaded for mercy. But it did little good. The pirates were teaching her, and the others watching, a valuable lesson.

For more than a week, the 20 surviving Vietnamese boat people endured this type of treatment. But on the eighth day, Ted Schweitzer showed up and rescued them, taking them to the Songkla Camp in Thailand.

#   #   #

Within three days of Schweitzer rescuing these Vietnamese, another boatload carrying 78 refugees left Nha Trang, Vietnam, on December 8, 1979. Their journey was uneventful until the third day, when they ran out of both food and fuel. For ten days the refugees' boat drifted aimlessly on the open sea, the people starving and nearly being driven mad by their miserable situation. Before anyone would discover them, twelve children would die.

On December 21 they were excited and relieved to spot two larger vessels sailing their way. Unbeknownst to the refugees, the two boats were pirate ships. Forcing all 66 of the Vietnamese onto their own boat, the pirates searched each one for valuables, taking from them whatever they desired. They then moved onto the tiny wooden ship and searched there too, prying up the wooden planks from the bottom, making sure nothing was hidden underneath.

One Vietnamese woman brought aboard the pirate ship was obviously pregnant and near collapse. For the past ten days, she, along with the others, had endured a nightmare. They were lost at sea, starving, and forced to watch as several of their children died.

Once this woman climbed aboard the pirate ship, she immediately crumbled to the deck, weak and unable to move. But one of the pirates quickly yanked her to her feet and demanded that she stand back up. The woman tried, but her legs simply could not hold her and she slid to the ground once again. This time, the pirate didn't even bother to yank her up, he simply beat the young pregnant woman viciously and violently, until she lay dead in a pool of blood and gore. Then he and a companion picked her up and threw her body overboard.

The pirates sailed their captives to Koh Kra Island, beating and abusing them throughout the entire trip. Upon reaching their destination they were taken ashore and again attacked and raped on an hourly basis. The next day two more pirate ships appeared and again beat and tortured the men while gang raping the women.

This time, however, the pirates had more in mind than just having their fun on the island. Taking the three prettiest girls with them, they forced two onto one pirate ship, and the other onto a second pirate ship. Although the two who left together would later be rescued in Songkla, where they had been taken to be sold as sex slaves, the third girl would never be seen or heard from again. To this day, her fate remains a mystery, although it is not hard to imagine what became of her.

#   #   #

Nearly every single week Schweitzer would get reports of people being stranded and held prisoner on Koh Kra Island, and each time he would travel out there to try to rescue them.

On December 31st, a pirate ship had come upon a boatload of 120 Vietnamese refugees, and rammed the tiny wooden vessel, cracking the structure and terrifying those aboard. Disabling their motor, the pirates then looted the boat and robbed the people. They took the prettiest girls back to their ship, and then rammed the wooden boat again, causing a massive hole that sunk the vessel in a matter of seconds.

Leaving the seventy people left on board to drown, the pirates took the fifty girls and sailed to Koh Kra. The next day, January 1, 1980, a Thai Navy ship appeared on the scene, and several naval officers came ashore. If the refugees had hopes that these men might help them, they were sadly mistaken. The sailors ordered them to strip naked and then stand in line at attention. Confused and embarrassed, the Vietnamese did what they were told, and after the officers looked each one over, they quickly departed.

The next day, a different Thai Navy boat appeared, and the routine was repeated. Each refugee was made to strip while the navy men looked them over and then left the island. But this fleet of men, unlike their predecessors, kept their navy ship anchored just off shore for the next two days.

All the while the navy ship sat there, no pirates had approached the island. But the moment the navy departed, on January 4, 1980 the pirates immediately re-appeared, swarming around the little atoll. Four pirate ships, loaded down with gangs of men, quickly came ashore and took turns savagely raping the women in front of all their family and friends.

But apparently this was not enough for the group. The men quickly rounded up five female children, ranging in age from 11 to 14, and brutally gang raped each. Luckily, their ordeal would only last one night. The very next day, January 5th, Ted Schweitzer showed up to rescue them.

#   #   #

Coming ashore of an island held by pirates was always a dangerous mission, and Schweitzer had his fair share of terrifying moments and outright fights. But nothing prepared him for his most perilous adventure yet.

On January 12, 1980, during a routine helicopter patrol, Schweitzer had seen dozens of half-naked Vietnamese on Koh Kra. He also spotted two Thai fishing boats, which he knew belonged to a notorious pirate gang, resting at anchor just off shore.

Typically, Schweitzer would have the Thai Marine Patrol escort him to the island whenever people were being held there, but on this particular day, none was available. Two days passed, and still Schweitzer found it impossible to secure a patrol to take him to Koh Kra. He knew he had to get out there, and being desperate, he approached the captain of an old fishing vessel.

Schweitzer offered to pay the man $500, out of his own pocket, to rent his boat and crew, and secure passage to Koh Kra. The captain agreed, and the ship set sail on the dark and stormy evening of January 14th, reaching the island near midnight. Schweitzer preferred to approach at night, in the hope of being less visible to the pirates on the atoll.

On this particular trip, the weather was bad. It was the monsoon season, and the air was frosty. As the boat approached the island, the seas continued to swell and churn. The waves seemed massive, rushing forward and crashing against the rocks of the little atoll. It was impossible to get close, and the captain dropped anchor 400 yards offshore, refusing to continue until daybreak.

As the boat rested quietly at anchor, its engines shut off, Schweitzer and the crew became aware of a cacophony coming from the island. It was a combination of banging, shouting, and high pitched, blood-curdling screams. Soon, they could see campfires being lit around shore, and Schweitzer knew the pirates were hunting down the hiding women and bringing them to the beach to be raped.

The men listened for several minutes, the time seeming to drag on endlessly, and then half an hour passed, and soon an hour, but still the noise did not subside. It was the sound of people, mainly women, terrified, wounded and in pain.

Unable to take it anymore, Schweitzer stripped to his underwear and dove off the deck of the fishing boat, much to the surprise of the others aboard. Hitting the water was like a thousand knives being plunged into his body, but Schweitzer barely noticed. All he could think of was getting to shore and helping those people caught in a nightmare. Using all his strength, he began to swim.

But the sea was choppy, and for every foot Schweitzer made, the giant swells seemed to push him back two. Within moments he was thoroughly exhausted, his limbs numb from the cold, yet aching dully from the effort it took to stay above water. He was scared at the thought of what he might find once he reached the atoll, but the adrenaline of his mission kept him going. Plowing through the surf, he finally saw the tiny island in sight. It had taken him an entire hour to traverse the four hundred yards.

The current was taking him where it pleased, and he had no control over where he was swimming. Eventually, he was thrashed against the rocks of a steep cliff on the western edge of the island. Pulling himself onto a jutting rock, Schweitzer soon found that the waves would not let him move any further. They pounded against him, battering his body over and over, and slamming it down upon the jagged rocks he clung to.

Eventually he was able to make his way up to a level ledge, but in the process his arms and legs were cut and slashed by the sharp stones. Now, totally exhausted and dismayed to see that the cliff in front of him rose nearly 200 feet in a vertical mass, Schweitzer wondered what he would do. He was bleeding heavily from his torn and tattered arms and legs, and he knew he would never have the strength to climb to the top. He worried now about his own survival, let alone that of the Vietnamese refugees.

Stunned and fatigued, he lay there for a while, just trying to catch his breath. Soon, however, he heard voices from the top of the cliff and called out to them. Two Vietnamese men peered over the edge and then began to descend. Upon seeing the battered Schweitzer, one of the two exclaimed, 'Oh we are saved!'

Taking off their pants, the Vietnamese men made a sling and hoisted Schweitzer up the cliff. Once on top, they tore strips from their shirts and made makeshift bandages to cover his wounds. Then they told him what was going on.

The refugees said that there were about 80 Vietnamese on the island, having survived the capsizing of their boat. They had been there for more than a week, with no food and very little water. The weather had gotten stormy, and two days ago, the 'robbers', (pirates) had arrived and came ashore. They had immediately attacked the shipwrecked bunch, killing several of the men by beating them to death or stabbing them with swords, and forcing the rest to flee into the jungle.

But the pirates had tracked down the women and girls and taken them to a lonely spot on the beach where they were raping and brutalizing them. Schweitzer, who was still exhausted, but who also felt a rush of adrenaline at the refugee's story, forced himself to his feet.

Telling the men to take him there, the three made their way through the jungle, to the other side of the rocky cliff. There, the men pointed to a spot overlooking the beach. As Schweitzer peered through the vegetation, he could see about fifty men, all pirates, systematically raping a group of young girls. Empty liquor bottles littered the area, and the men were laughing and clapping, slurring their words as they shouted encouragement to their comrades. It was evident that the 'party' had been going on for some time, and the pirates were dead drunk.

Schweitzer knew he could do nothing alone, and he asked the Vietnamese men where the others were hiding. The men told him that other women were, hiding in the jungle and in caves, while the men were together, in a clearing a short distance away.

Schweitzer directed the men to take him there, which they did, showing him 35 bedraggled and terrified men and boys. Some of them held crudely made weapons of wood and stone, but Schweitzer didn't think any of them would have the strength to use them. Still, he knew that they must take action now, or those women with the pirates were as good as dead.

"We have to help the women." He said, seeing a new expression of fear leap into their eyes.

One of the men shook his head in resignation. "We can't," he said, "they are too well-armed."

Schweitzer shook his head and said confidently, "They'll listen to me."

The appearance of Ted Schweitzer, followed meekly by thirty-five Vietnamese men, caught the pirates by surprise. Jumping up off the women they quickly banded together, brandishing an array of weapons including pistols, knives, axes and lead pipes.

In a loud, stern voice, Schweitzer shouted that he worked for the United Nations and that the Vietnamese were under his protection. Then he ordered the pirates to leave the island directly.

The pirates shouted for the men to get back, but Schweitzer was afraid to do so, fearing that if they retreated, the pirates would attack before they could reach the safety of the jungle. Instead, Schweitzer held his ground, telling the group that if they killed the Vietnamese refugees, no one would care. "But I am a U.N. official." He said, "If you kill me, they'll look for me, they'll find me, and they'll hunt you down.

The pirates laughed, but it was a nervous sound, and many of them began backing down the beach, away from Schweitzer and his men. The Vietnamese, seeing that the pirates were intimidated, now swarmed around their protector and begin swinging their clubs at the retreating group.

The girls and women, some having been raped so violently that they could no longer walk and had to drag themselves across the beach, quickly darted into the jungle and hid.

The pirates immediately moved into counterattack mode and advanced on the men ominously. One of them, carrying a lead pipe, went after Schweitzer, viciously clubbing him across the face and head.

Schweitzer went down, and more pirates joined the melee on him, clubbing him, kicking him and punching him. The lone man did what he could to fight back but it was a futile attempt and he knew it. He curled himself into a ball, trying to protect his most vulnerable parts, until he passed out.

The pirates continued the beating, even after the man lost consciousness, and didn't stop until he was half dead. They had broken his rib, his shoulder, and beaten his head to bruised and battered pulp. But they did not kill him. Instead, they fled the island, but kept their boats resting just off shore.

When Schweitzer finally regained consciousness, he was dizzy, lightheaded, and in a tremendous amount of pain. His shoulder throbbed like a rotted tooth, and his side, where his rib was broken, made it almost impossible to breathe. More alarming yet was the fact that when he urinated, his urine was a pinkish red color. He would find that the beating had so severely injured his kidney that he would require medical attention for the rest of his life.

Gathered all around him were panic stricken Vietnamese, begging him for help, and terrified that the pirates were still out there and might return at any moment. Trying to clear his head, his vision blurred, Schweitzer scanned the horizon and was thankful to see the fishing vessel he had arrived on still sitting 400 yards offshore.

But his happiness soon faded as he wondered how they would ever reach it. The seas had not calmed down, so the boat could not approach any closer, and the pirates were still sitting there at anchor, watching closely.

But Schweitzer couldn't worry about that now. He was in unbelievable pain, and his head pounded like a sledgehammer. Crawling further up the beach, he positioned himself on a cool bed of grass, at the edge of the jungle, and rested.

He must have dozed off, because the next thing he knew, he was surrounded by a total of 88 Vietnamese men, women and children, each staring at him with a look of concern on their faces. Immediately, the women were kneeling next to him, wiping the dried blood from his face and head. The others, including the men, were taking off their clothes and ripping them into pieces, creating makeshift bandages for his wounds. Taking several of these, Schweitzer bound up his sore ribs and allowed the refugees to care for him.

But he was relieved to see that the pirate ships were now gone, and he knew they could wait no longer. Many of those on the island, himself included, needed medical attention, and still he wondered how they would return to the ship. Having no other alternative, Schweitzer lined up the 88 refugees, and creating a human chain, the mass of people began to swim to the waiting fishing boat.

The task was slow, extremely painful, and seemed to take forever. But eventually the large group made it to the boat and were hauled aboard. Then the small, dangerously overloaded ship set sail for Songkla, Thailand,   for   help.

Chapter Four

Once Ted Schweitzer recovered enough from his beating, he paid another visit to the Thai government and was again rebuffed. The Thai officials told Schweitzer that they believed many of the Vietnamese had made up the horror stories of what happened to them in an effort to gain sympathy. Angered, Schweitzer appealed to the U.N, and the United States Navy, for help.

The United Nations was appalled by what had happened to him and the refugees, and they provided him with money, equipment, and bodyguards. As a U.N. official, Schweitzer was forbidden to carry a firearm, but his bodyguards were allowed to arm themselves, which would be of tremendous help.

In April, a U.S. reconnaissance aircraft flying out of the Philippines spotted a large group of people on Koh Kra. Relaying this information to the U.S. Embassy in Bangkok, they in turn informed Schweitzer at the UNHCR.

Schweitzer enlisted the help of two policemen to sail with him to the island on a fishing boat, where they arrived at around 7:00 am. Once onshore, the Vietnamese told them that approximately 40 Thai fishermen had taken several of their women into the jungle and were raping them.

Schweitzer immediately began giving directives to surround the group in the thick vegetation, but one of the policemen instantly balked. He would not leave the beach he insisted. The other officer, however, was willing to help, and managed to flush several of the pirates, along with two teenage girls they were brutalizing, out of the jungle. For Schweitzer, the trip was a success. He returned to the mainland of Thailand with four pirates he had placed under arrest.

The Thai government was incensed about this 'American' arresting their citizens, and they challenged Schweitzer's right to do so. Infuriated, Schweitzer told them he had the authority of 'international law on the high seas administered by the International Court of Justice in The Hague'. That was enough to shut the officials up for the moment, but Schweitzer was quickly becoming a problem that the Thai government didn't care to deal with anymore.

#   #   #

Schweitzer couldn't have cared less about what the Thai government thought of him. He had no intention of stopping what he was doing. He couldn't. His heart literally broke for the plight of the Vietnamese boat people, and he was determined to do whatever he could for them.

Time after time he returned to the island of Koh Kra and rescued kidnapped and shipwrecked refugees. Often, he would be forced to battle it out with the pirates who held them, at one time getting stabbed in the hip and another time shot in arm. The treatment these people suffered never varied, it remained constant and brutal.

The total number of those Ted Schweitzer rescued reached 500, 800, one thousand and more, and still the Vietnamese boat people continued to be attacked, kidnapped, raped, beaten, robbed, and killed.

On what was to be his last mission, although he was not aware of that, Schweitzer encountered a brutal band of pirates raping a number of refugee girls. Some of these girls were little more than children, and the sight enraged the U.N. official. Advancing on the group, a violent fight broke out and Schweitzer was once again fighting for his life.

But he managed to arrest seven of the pirates, all of them Thai fishermen, and return them to their country for prosecution. 'It was seven more', Schweitzer would quip, 'than the Thai government had arrested in all the time he had been going to Koh Kra.'

It was also the proverbial straw that broke the camel's back. For it was shortly after this that all hell broke loose.

#   #   #

The Thai government had had enough of Ted Schweitzer, and so had many of the citizens of Thailand. It wasn't so much that they endorsed what the pirates were doing, but the majority of them were desperately poor Thai fisherman, and piracy was simply too great a temptation for them to resist. They understood this, and had no desire to see Thai citizens being imprisoned for crimes against the Vietnamese, a country they held no sympathy for.

But it was no longer so easy for the Thai government to just turn a blind eye to what was happening over on Koh Kra. Schweitzer's rescues had finally grabbed the media's attention, and the plight of the Vietnamese boat people was being aired all over the world. Thailand was coming under heavy criticism for their lack of response to the problem, and Schweitzer was being lauded as a hero for his efforts.

There was little that could have riled the Thai government more, or its citizens for that matter. Schweitzer needed to go, and fast. He was threatened numerous times, and relatives of the seven pirates he had arrested were reported to have taken a contract out on his life. But Schweitzer didn't care, nor was he afraid.

He soon found out, however, that the Thai government wasn't afraid either. Even with the press watching, they notified the United Nations High Commissioner for Refugees and told them that Theodore Schweitzer was no longer welcome to serve in Thailand.

The outright banning of Schweitzer from working in Thailand threatened to cause a media storm for the country that had the potential to disrupt their entire kingdom. But the Thai government didn't care. They wanted Schweitzer out, and gone for good, immediately. They did, however, relent just a bit by publicly announcing that while he was no longer allowed to engage in any type of work in the country, they would welcome him as a visitor.

Schweitzer knew his wife, a Thai native, would be happy about that, but he wondered what he would do now. With his work apparently over there, in May of 1980, Schweitzer reluctantly accepted a transfer to the UNHCR headquarters in Geneva.

Twice during his time there he was rushed into emergency surgery for the injuries his kidneys had sustained. His time fighting pirates in the South China Sea had done its damage, and with his health failing, in 1983 he took a medical retirement from the civil service.

Now, still young, but prematurely retired, Schweitzer returned to the states and settled in Florida. His parents lived there, and he thought it might be a good place to recuperate and decide what he was going to do with the rest of his life.

If Ted Schweitzer was unsure of where his future might lead him, it came as no surprise to others that his work with the Vietnamese people was far from over.

Chapter Five

The country of Thailand may have thought that by getting rid of Ted Schweitzer, their problems with the refugees and pirates would fade into obscurity. But they would quickly realize that it was not going to be that easy. Schweitzer continued to bring attention to the plight of the Vietnamese boat people and the horrors they endured, and he made frequent trips back to Thailand.

In 1982, Ted Schweitzer co-founded the SEA RESCUE FOUNDATION, a non-profit organization dedicated to assisting refugees, prisoners or war, and others in distress throughout Asia, Indo-China and elsewhere. Sea Rescue provided food, housing, medical care, and protection for those in need, and rescue at sea to hundreds of thousands of people.

Schweitzer's dream for SEA RESCUE was to create a multi-national maritime patrol force to guard the South China Sea and the coasts of Thailand and Malaysia. He attributed the majority of the piracy on the gulf to the large number of fishing vessels, and the gross lack of marine patrol boats. He believed the solution to the problem was to set up a system of boats to pick up the refugees before they reached the waters sailed by pirates.

'If you fly over the gulf at night', he said, 'it looks like a city with all the fishermen's boats. When a refugee boat sails into that city of fishermen, sooner or later they are going to get raped. What would happen in any city of 200,000 without any policemen?'

But no matter how much he tried to fulfill his dream, others were not interested in participating in it, nor did they share the same passion that Schweitzer felt for his Vietnamese boat people.

Reluctantly, Schweitzer realized that he needed to cast about for an alternative solution to solving the problem of the Vietnamese boat people. Although SEA RESCUE had originally been created with the boat people in mind, Schweitzer always knew that the organization could be of value to those on land also. Now he wondered, could he use SEA RESCUE in the country in Vietnam itself?

Schweitzer knew in his heart that the only real way to end the piracy on the South China Sea was for the Vietnamese to stay in Vietnam. He believed that if he could help to improve the living conditions there, the refugee's would not want to leave. They were the ones who needed to make Vietnam the great country they wanted it to be.

'If I were Vietnamese,' Schweitzer declared, 'I'd stay in Vietnam.'

#   #   #

At the end of the Vietnam War in the early 1970's, there were 2,583 American troops listed as being missing. In the spring 1973, at the end of Operation Homecoming, only 591 POWs were returned, along with the remains of another 113 who had died in captivity. And from that moment on the American public demanded to know what had happened to those that were unaccounted for.

Since 1975, the United States had been trying to answer this question, sending delegates to Vietnam to gather what information they could on these missing men. President Jimmy Carter sent a man in 1977, but it would be President Ronald Reagan who really pushed for an answer.

In the early 1980's Reagan sent an Ambassador to Hanoi on three separate occasions to inquire as to the fate of American MIA's. In 1987 he appointed General John Vessey as President Emissary to Hanoi on the MIA issue.

Although Vietnam was quick to tell the United States that it had no information on missing American servicemen, Vessey knew they were lying. Occasionally the country would release personal items that could only have come from the missing men. Family photos, identification cards, personal letters, and American money, among other things. When asked where these items came from, the Vietnamese officials would never give a straight answer.

Vessey wasn't one to tiptoe around the issues, and he was prepared to force the answers from the Vietnamese, but he needed some type of proof that the Vietnam government couldn't deny. What Vessey needed was something to use against them, to compel them to relay whatever information they had about American MIA's.

Malcolm McConnell, who was chief of the MIA/POW office, had told Vessey that what he needed to get were the secret files and archives from the Vietnamese government. Vessey had no idea whether such records still existed or not, but he wanted an accounting of those left behind after the war, and he asked McConnell how he could acquire them.

McConnell suggested recruiting a Vietnam official as a spy. Vessey liked the idea, but he also knew that this was much easier said than done. The chances of either man actually finding someone to do the dirty work was practically nil.

One day, in 1987 or 1988, McConnell met Ted Schweitzer and discussed with him their need to get into the Vietnamese archives. Ted had asked a few questions, and then the conversation had moved on to other topics. The two men visited for a while, and then Schweitzer left. McConnell didn't think about their conversation again, nor did he mention Schweitzer to General Vessey. There simply was no reason to.

#   #   #

In August of 1988, Ted Schweitzer returned to Indochina. But instead of focusing on the Vietnamese boat people, he used his SEA RESCUE Foundation to bring donated medical supplies and equipment to the people still living in Vietnam.

Schweitzer was worried about how he might be received in the country, but he need not have been. The Foreign Ministry of the Socialist Republic of Vietnam greeted him happily when he arrived in Hanoi. He was well known for the work he had done with the boat people, and his Foreign Ministry escort, Ambassador Nguyen Can, truly believed that Schweitzer would bring needed assistance to his war torn country.

As Schweitzer visited more and more often, each time bringing desperately needed supplies, the Vietnamese of Hanoi began to welcome him like a hero. And he was a hero to them. He was the man who risked his life for the boat people of their country, and was now helping to save their sick and injured. Ted Schweitzer soon became something of a savior to the people of Vietnam.

In July of 1989, Schweitzer again returned to Hanoi, bringing with him thousands of dollars in medical supplies for a new pediatric hospital in Hah Nam Ninh Province. He was again greeted warmly, and spent several weeks in the country.

When he returned to the states, Schweitzer traveled to the Pentagon and paid a visit to his old friend Malcolm McConnell. Walking into his office, Schweitzer dropped two rolls of film on his desk and told him that he might be interested in them. The two men chatted for a while, and then Schweitzer left.

Curious, McConnell had the film developed and was shocked by what he saw. The pictures were of index cards listing items recovered from a crash site of American men still missing. Each card was dated, and named the location from which the items were recovered. Each listed item was numbered and described.

Picking up the phone, McConnell immediately called Ted Schweitzer and asked him what he was looking at.

"You're looking at the Vietnamese archives." Ted replied.

McConnell was stunned. What the American government, with all its money and resources, had not been able to access in almost twenty years, Ted Schweitzer had done in little more than one trip to Hanoi. How was such a thing possible?

Schweitzer explained that he had become familiar with secret and sensitive archives while working as a media consultant at the American Air Force Base in Udorn back in the 1970's. He had a good idea of what McConnell needed, and he knew exactly what to look for.

Telling the Vietnamese that he wanted to write a book about American POW's, but from the Vietnamese perspective, not the American, Schweitzer asked if they could help him with records and documents.

The Vietnamese were quick to agree, having only one stipulation; Schweitzer would have to pay them for their time doing the research. Schweitzer had immediately agreed, and the very next day the men had brought the files that McConnell was looking at.

These documents would be only the first of many that Schweitzer photographed and brought back to McConnell. On subsequent trips, he gained access to the Central Military Museum in Hanoi and took pictures of hundreds of others. He was instrumental in getting not only proof that Vietnam knew much more about American MIA's than they were willing to admit, but also information as to what actually happened to many of those servicemen who never came home from the war.

To the families of these missing men who had agonized over their fate for two decades or more, closure was the best gift Ted Schweitzer could have given them.

Afterword

The little island of Koh Kra holds many secrets, and probably some ghosts too. By October of 1980, 160 refugees were known to have died there, a number that many believe is pitifully inaccurate. To most, the number is much, much, higher than that.

In 1981 the United States stationed a detail of eight Marines to guard the island, finally ending the pirate's use of it as their personal playground. But piracy on the South China Sea continued anyway, all throughout the 1980's.

In 1981 the UNHCR won the Nobel Peace Prize for their humanitarian efforts in the plight of the Vietnamese boat people. Leaders at the U.N. sent Ted Schweitzer a replica of the prize, which he proudly displays on his office wall.

By the latter half of the 1980's the Thai government was trying to improve their image, regarding piracy within their waters, by putting into effect certain laws to protect those refugees sailing the open seas.

They ordered all fishing boats to prominently display numbers on the prow of their ships, and also installed cameras to photograph any boat going in or out of port.

While this may have deterred some of the pirates, it had the opposite effect on others. Many now became far more brutal, killing every refugee they came upon in an attempt to avoid leaving witnesses. One Thai citizen would later talk about how Vietnamese women used to be kidnapped and then brought to the mainland. There, they would be sold to brothels to work as prostitutes. 'Now', the man said, 'the women are still kidnapped, but it is too risky to bring them to the mainland. So when the men are finished with them...' Here, the man finished his sentence with a shrug of his shoulders.

Even though piracy continued, Thailand was quick to state that statistically, there was a drastic decline in the number of refugee boats being attacked by them. Ted Schweitzer publicly called this statement 'bullshit'. He believed the government bureaucrats were deliberately fudging the numbers to allow them to appear in a better light. 'They just keep telling their lies,' he said, 'it just washes the blood off their hands a little bit'.

By this time the U.N. was overseeing a 15 million dollar anti-piracy program funded by the United States and ten other countries. They increased patrols at sea and investigations on land, and they too were claiming that the number of attacks on refugees had drastically been reduced.

Schweitzer disagreed, saying that 'Nobody likes to admit that piracy is still going on. They'd rather hide their heads in the sand'. It was a statement that the Vietnamese refugees completely agreed with.

What the Vietnamese boat people suffered is difficult to comprehend, and the statistics regarding these displaced persons stagger the mind. Most of those who endured these horrors believe the numbers are woefully below reality.

It is estimated that 60% of all women between the ages of 9 and 56 were raped while on the gulf, and according to the Vietnam Women's Association of San Jose, another 3500 were sold into sex slavery.

From 1975 to 1986, the UNHCR estimates that 200,000 to 250,000 Vietnamese boat people died at sea. This figure does not include those refugees murdered by pirates on Koh Kra Island. Nor does it include all those who are not accounted for. The number of those missing are estimated to be around 60,000. But when one considers that pirates, at times, would sink or kill entire boatloads of refugees, leaving no one alive to report them as missing, these numbers may be drastically incorrect.

By the late 1980's many of the refugees who had survived their ordeal were beginning to speak publicly of what they had endured. In 1987 Cam Nhung told reporters how 20 pirates had raped her for 20 hours, while her small daughter looked on. Others spoke of being passed from Thai fishing ship to Thai fishing ship and raped for days on end.

For many of these survivors, the wounds never healed. Suicides and suicide attempts among the Vietnamese boat people are often quite high.

And still the Thai government remained protective of their fishermen turned pirates. Between 1975 and 1985, Thai officials prosecuted fewer than 70 men for the crime of piracy. And for as much as they liked to claim that piracy attacks in the South China Sea had dwindled, in 1986 alone there were 141 documented attacks which left 132 people dead or missing, 142 women raped, and 64 abducted. Out of the 64 missing, only 14 were ever recovered.

To be fair, there were some refugees who spoke of encountering Thai fishermen who were kind to them, ones that didn't molest them and provided them with food and water. But the number of these reports were few and far between.

Through all of this Ted Schweitzer remained a hero and a true humanitarian. Nhat Tien, one of the original 157 boat people Schweitzer rescued from Koh Kra, went on to become one of the most respected authors in the Vietnamese language, and said of Schweitzer, 'He's a great man. He rescued a lot of people.' And Nguyen Huu Xuong, director of the Boat People SOS Committee in San Diego says 'He's a fantastic man.'

Today, Schweitzer continues to operate his SEA RESCUE foundation, an organization that has helped thousands of people through its effort. He took scores of pictures of the Vietnamese refugees on Koh Kra Island, many of which can be seen on the SEA RESCUE website.

But Ted Schweitzer never received the recognition he deserved, neither for his work with the Vietnamese boat people, nor his help with the MIA issue in Vietnam. According to his own estimates, he saved more than 1200 Vietnamese from the hands of evil and despicable men. But there are many who feel that's a conservative number. In truth, his rescues might total as many as 3,000 or more. His name should be a household word, yet few people even know he exists.

The refugees and others he has helped know, though. On the abandoned lighthouse on Koh Kra, where the refugees had written a warning about the pirates, there now rests a plaque dedicated to him. It is a truly fitting tribute to a man who risked his life in an effort to save people he didn't even know:

IN HONOR OF THE THOUSANDS OF REFUGEES

WHO WERE MAROONED, ABUSED, TORTURED
AND EVEN MURDERED

HERE ON KOH KRA ISLAND. MAY THEIR
SUFFERING NEVER BE

FORGOTTEN. WITH HEARTFELT THANKS TO
MR. TED SCHWEITZER

WHO WAS INSTRUMENTAL IN SAVING
THOUSANDS OF MAROONED

REFUGEES.

Bibliography

www.miafacts.org/hanoi.html

www.searescue.org/SEARESCUEFOUNDATION.aspx

www.vietnamexodus.info/vne/forgetmenot/oneman.html

www.refugeecamps.net/kohkrainto.html

www.pbs.org/wgbh/amex/vietnam/trenches/mia.html

books.google.com/books?id=ZI5s5eS4_LQC&pg=PA168&dq=ted+schweitzer+vietnamese+boat+people+source=bl&oys=j2qOiyYwoR&sig=OGDIAPaQUjAT7yleU5a

news.google.com/newspapers?nid=1901&dat=19880805&id=vIwfAAAAIBAJ&sjid=UdMEAAAAIBAJ&pg=2925,2425222

The Orange County Register May 22, 1987

The San Diego Union Tribune July 20, 1986

Inside Hanoi's Secret Archives by Malcolm McConnell with Theodore G Schweitzer copyright 1995 Simon and Shuster Publishing

Made in USA

One Man's Dream to Manufacture Cheap Clothes...At All Costs

By Reagan Martin

Prologue

'*Sweatshops*'- it's a word that conjures up dark images of small children sitting behind sewing machines, working long hours for very little pay, in dull and dirty factories. The word first originated in the mid 1800's to describe just those conditions, at a time when these factories flourished in such places as Great Britian and New York City. These places earned the name 'sweatshop' for the brutally hot conditions under which the employees were forced to work.

Throughout the years, many tragedies occurred in these sweatshops, but probably none more tragic than the fire that struck the Triangle Shirtwaist Factory in New York City on March 25, 1911. The factory occupied the top three floors of a ten story building in Greenwich Village near Washington Square Park. On that March day, managers had locked the exits and stairwells to prevent the employees from taking unauthorized breaks. Around 4:30 in the afternoon, a fire broke out and quickly turned into a raging inferno. With the stairwells and exits blocked, workers could not get out of the building. When they realized they were trapped, many of them began jumping out of the top floor windows. By the time the fire was brought under control, a total of 146 people had perished.

The fire finally brought attention to the sweatshops operating in the city, and legislation was quickly passed to ensure better safety standards in the workplace. It was also this incident that led to the formation of International Ladies Garment Workers Union which continues to fight for better working conditions to this day.

Little by little things improved for immigrants coming to both America and Great Britain, and sweatshops eventually came to be a thing of the past, although this does not mean that they no longer exist in places such as the U.S. and the U.K.

The word sweatshop is defined as 'working long hours for low pay in below standard conditions' so technically, those wealthy residents who hire illegal aliens to work in their homes and fields, for less than minimum wage, could be said to be operating 'sweatshops.' Although most people don't view them that way.

Those sweatshops that people envision when they hear the word do exist however, mostly in third world countries such as China, Vietnam and Thailand. Here, very young children, as well as men and women of all ages, are still employed to work long hours for extremely low pay.

It is an ongoing problem that most people attribute to nothing more than greed. But there are two views to every situation. While many support bringing an end to the sweatshops of the world, there are a surprising number of people who defend them. And they are not just the factory owners, but many of the people who work in them too.

Those who live in these third world countries toil long and hard anyway, and often for far less money than they can make in a sweatshop. In many respects, to lose these jobs in the factories would make their lives far more difficult.

For an American, to hear that a sweatshop worker was being paid .30 cents an hour for a 60 hour workweek, might sound like modern day slavery. But when one considers that the average pay for this same person in their own country is $1.00 a day, it doesn't sound so bad to be making $3.00 a day in a sweatshop.

In 1993 Tom Harkin, an Iowa Senator, proposed banning imports from any country that used children in sweatshops. This may have seemed like a wonderful idea, but as a result of it, the country of Bangladesh laid off 50,000 children. And, according to Oxfam, a leading British charity, a large number of these children were forced to become prostitutes in order to earn a living and survive.

It is for just these reasons that many people from poor countries still accept jobs in factories they know will be labelled sweatshops. They've heard the horror stories, but they're used to working long hours anyway, and for less pay, and in less than perfect conditions. They assume they might face harsher restrictions and less freedom, and they're willing too. In truth, they firmly believe it won't be all that much different from their current lives.

Of course, none of them had ever worked for Kil Soo Lee before, but that didn't matter. They were certain he wasn't operating a sweatshop anyway.

Chapter One

When 48-year-old South Korean Kil Soo Lee chose the Pacific island of American Samoa to house his new garment factory, it seemed, too many, like a dream come true. Lee portrayed himself as a kind and generous businessman, eager to hire those less privileged than himself. He wanted to offer hard-working people, those who struggled daily because of pitifully low wages, a new start at life.

The majority of Lee's work force would be made up of young females, comprised of Samoan, Vietnamese and Chinese nationals. Girls who would sew clothing - sporting attire, jackets, and swimsuits - at The Daewoosa Samoa Garment Factory LTD. These goods would then be exported to the United States, and other countries, to be sold in such stores such as JC Penney, Sears and Target.

Officials on American Samoa believed Lee's new factory would benefit both their residents, and their stagnant economy, and they were happy to have him. The country of Vietnam felt the same way.

Lee was promising his Vietnamese workers a monthly salary of $400, regardless if work was available for them or not. In a country where 80% of the population was made up of farmers who averaged an annual salary of just $200 per year, this was an astronomical amount of money. But for the Vietnamese hierarchy, there was an added bonus. They could charge their citizens a high fee just for the opportunity to work at the factory and for the documentation needed to leave their country.

For the government of Vietnam, it was a win/win situation. Potential employees could be charged $3,000 to $8,000 to secure the job, guaranteeing the government a huge profit on this fee alone, and of course once the person was actually working, most of their pay would undoubtedly be sent back home where it would quickly be introduced into the country's struggling economy. How could the Vietnamese government lose?

But it wasn't just American Samoa and Vietnam that were happy about the situation, the United States was pleased with it as well. Just like Puerto Rico, American Samoa, which is located 2300 miles south of Hawaii, is an unincorporated territory of the United States. It is not a state, nor are its residents considered American citizens, but the little island shares a close relationship with its parent country. Although the Samoans cannot vote in U.S. elections, its government is modeled after America's, and they have an elected delegate to the U.S. Congress. In addition, any elected President to the United States automatically becomes the head of state on American Samoa.

Because of these close ties, a factory on the island could be of great benefit to the U.S. Materials used in the manufacture of the clothing could be sent directly from the mainland, thereby enabling the factory to create stateside standard clothing which could then carry the 'Made in the USA' label. And because of the cost efficiency of creating the garments on the island, where the minimum wage was half of that in the states, the U.S. would be able to sell the clothing at highly competitive prices. Also saving thousands of dollars was the fact that goods made in American Samoa are not subjected to U.S. import quotas and tariffs.

All in all, the new Daewoosa Samoa Garment Factory seemed to be a great thing for people everywhere. When it opened its doors for business in 1998, hundreds of people had high hopes that it would change their lives forever. Unfortunately, they were right.

****

Dung Nguyen was a young, pretty Vietnamese girl, married and living with her husband and small daughter, when she first heard about the wonderful job that paid such good wages. Her next door neighbor brought an advertisement to show her, and as Dung read it, she thought it sounded almost too good to be true. A factory job in America, offering free room and board, plus a salary of $100 a week whether work was available or not? Dung simply couldn't believe it.

But it was obvious her neighbor believed it as she chattered on enthusiastically, thrusting the advertisement into the young girl's hands. Dung listened quietly to what her friend had to say, but she remained skeptical. She had heard horror stories of people taking 'fabulous' jobs, only to end up working in a 'sweatshop,' thousands of miles from home. Dung had no desire to become employed in one herself.

But her neighbor scoffed at her worries. "Not here," she said, "this job is in America. There are no sweatshops there."

Dung took the advertisement home and later that night she and her husband sat down to discuss it. Although both knew that there were pro's and con's to the job, each agreed it was certainly an opportunity worth considering. The money was exceptional, and the chance to work in America was like a dream come true. In America, even the poorest of people seemed rich too most.

But the job required a guarantee of three year's work from anyone interested in taking it, and Dung would have to leave her young daughter and husband behind. That was a long time for her to be away, living all alone in a strange country, and she worried about the sacrifice her husband would be making too. Their roles would have to be reversed; while she worked, he would have to stay home to care for their only child.

Although there was a lot to consider, the young couple found themselves relegating the cons to the bottom of the list. They found it difficult to move past the lure of such good money, and the more they spoke about it the more excited they became.

Further inquiries put a damper on things however, when Dung learned that she would have to pay a fee before taking the job, and a hefty fee at that. The price for her to go to work in America would cost Dung and her family $6,000. Money the Nguyen's simply did not have.

But even this was easily remedied, the Vietnamese labor officials told them. They could borrow the money from family, friends, or even a bank, and if that didn't work out there were always 'wealthy' people willing to help. Although the actual word for these wealthy people was never used, the Nguyen's were well aware that the officials were talking about loan sharks.

For almost a week, the young couple fretted over what they should do, and in the end they decided the job was simply too good to pass up. Just the chance to work and live in the United States was worth more than they could put a price on, and although they would miss each other, they felt the time would pass quickly.

Reasoning that over the course of the three years, Dung would earn a minimum of $14,400 - and possibly a lot more if she were able to take on other part time work during her off hours at the factory – both she and her husband believed that any sacrifice would be worth the reward. With that kind of money, even after paying back the initial fee, they would still see a profit of 8 to 10 thousand dollars. At Vietnamese wages, it might take them more than 40 *years* to earn that kind of money. With their decision finally made, Dung made preparations to leave for America, and others all over her country were doing the same.

Vietnamese job recruiters had offered 36-year-old Hoang Trong Thuy and his 33-year-old wife Nguyen Thi Ngoc, the chance to earn a staggering $36,000 for only three years' work at the Daewoosa Garment Factory in 'America.' Blinded by such a lucrative opportunity, just as so many others were, the couple quickly made arrangements to leave their four children behind and borrowed $11,000 from loan sharks to secure the job.

Throughout Vietnam, more than 200 people made the same decision, and none of them were unaware of the risks they took to do so. They borrowed money from family, friends and loan sharks, with no guarantee that they would ever be able to pay it back, and they willingly left behind everything that ever mattered to them. It was undeniable proof of just how bad things were in their own country.

Although it was a scary time for everyone, those who left were infused by an indomitable spirit and a burning desire to improve their lot in life. Things *would* work out, they assured themselves. They were travelling to the United States after all, where they would live and work in idyllic conditions and earn a small fortune. They were happy and excited by the opportunity, and despite all the risks, they truly believed it would all be worth it.

****

On the day Dung Nguyen was to travel to her new job in the United States, she dressed herself carefully, in a white blouse and new blue jeans, and packed her belongings in a small plastic suitcase. She not only wanted to look nice for her trip, but she wanted to look like an American.

At the airport, she kissed her husband and daughter goodbye, and then boarded the plane that would take her to her new job, and a brighter future for her family. The plane touched down in Honolulu Hawaii, where Dung boarded a second plane in a connecting flight. Later that day, she arrived at her destination, the island of American Samoa, 5,000 miles from her home and family.

As Dung exited the plane, she still believed that she had arrived in the United States, but she began to worry almost immediately. Why was the airport so small and empty, she wondered? It seemed odd because she had seen pictures of the massive airports in the U.S., and they always appeared to be jammed with mobs of rushing people. The weather wasn't what she expected either. Stepping outside of the air-conditioned building, the hot, sticky, humid heat assured Dung that she was still in the tropics and not in North America.

There was a bus waiting to take the women out to their new job at Daewoosa Garment Factory, and Dung climbed aboard, noticing the puzzled expressions on her fellow travelers and new co-workers. It seemed obvious that their final destination had not met their expectations either.

Reaching the factory, Dung saw a huge warehouse style building made of corrugated metal with a shiny tin roof. The blazing sun, which glared off of it, blinded her and hurt her eyes. All around the building, encircling the entire compound, was a high fence topped by razor wire in several sections. There was a guard shack at the entrance, and Dung could see a man's glaring face peering out at them. It reminded her of a maximum security prison, and she was instantly afraid.

When she was led into the warehouse and up to her dormitory, Dung's heart sank. The place looked like a barn with too many people haphazardly shoved inside. The smell was stomach turning; a combination of human waste, moldy clothing, and body odor. Strung all across the room were clotheslines with shirts, pants, socks and underwear hanging from them. The air was thick, heavy and sweltering. Sweat pour off people's faces and saturated their shirts. Rodent feces covered the floors and the beds, an inch or more thick in places. There were no screens on any of the windows, and the place literally buzzed with bumping insects floating about. There were no sinks, no hot water, no soap, and no toilet paper in sight. A dilapidated and disgustingly filthy shower stood in one corner of the room.

Dung stood frozen in place, drinking in the sight. She wanted to turn and run, to flee back to Vietnam and her husband and daughter. But she had already been warned that if she quit or left, or got herself deported, she would be fined an additional $5,000. She realized that the entire thing had been a fraud, a scam, a misrepresentation. She had been reluctant to apply because of the horror stories she had heard about sweatshops, and now it looked like she was going to be living in one.

Finally, Dung spoke. "Is this where we're going to live?" She asked in a trembling voice.

The man who had escorted them up to the dormitories gave her a little shove.

"Of course." He answered coldly, turning around to leave.

When he was finally gone, the other female workers approached Dung. This was a ritual they went through every time new arrivals appeared. They knew the girls who came had been duped, just like they had been duped when they first came, and they offered what little comfort they could. Dung looked so tiny, and so terrified, that the others finally offered her what they considered the dormitory's best bed. It was a top bunk, with a thin foam mattress, and they brought her a small wooden box to keep her belongings in. The bunk was considered the best because Dung would be allowed to sleep in it alone, as most of the women slept two to a bed, but more so because it was up high. Up there, the rats that came every night to chew through the women's mattresses and clothing, wouldn't be able to reach her.

Dung climbed up onto her bunk and began to cry. She was weary and exhausted after her long trip, but it was still several hours before she dozed off.

Chapter Two

For two full weeks Dung sweltered in the dormitory with nothing to do. She didn't know why she wasn't put to work, but she wished she had been. Being alone with her thoughts, feeling nauseous from the stench that emanated throughout the building and permeated the very clothes everyone wore, Dung found herself utterly miserable; and scared, very, very scared. She was hearing horror stories about the Daewoosa Factory that she found hard to believe.

She learned that although the workers were allowed to leave the fenced in compound once their shifts ended, they had a 10:00 pm curfew, and woe be it to anyone who broke curfew. If you were late coming back you were either slapped, beaten or abused. You were searched each time you left the factory and each time you returned, and often personal items were confiscated and never returned. At other times, if the owner was concerned about something, the factory would go on lockdown and no one was allowed to leave.

She was told not to count on anything that had been promised to her before she came here. They were supposed to work an eight hour day and get paid overtime for anything beyond 40 hours a week, but that never happened. Sometimes they were forced to work 18 hour workdays for a month or more, and then would be given no work for weeks at a time. They were never paid for this either, even though they had been assured they would be paid whether work was available or not.

Dung also learned very quickly to be careful when taking a shower in her dormitory. The first day she did, she found herself standing ankle deep in a pool of human feces, and even more startling, her boss stood outside the stall, leering at her naked body. The toilets constantly backed up into the showers, and the factory owner, along with several of the guards, regularly watched the young women as they took showers and got dressed.

Although Daewoosa Factory employed Vietnamese, Chinese and Samoan nationals, of the 313 employee's there, 251 were Vietnamese, and 90% of all the workers were women. They had all come to this place with the same hopes and dreams and excitement, and each of them had those feelings shattered in an instant.

Dung was allowed to write letters home, and make phone calls when she was outside the compound, and she wrote to her family all the time. She told them how much she missed them, and how much she loved them, but she was careful not to reveal how truly awful things were for her. She didn't want to burden them with any added worry. She figured they were probably worried enough already.

After two weeks, Dung was brought into the factory and placed behind a sewing machine. The work came non-stop, and it was so stifling hot in the huge metal building that the temperature soared to 100 degrees and beyond. The constant running of the machines added to the heat, and contributed to the stench already hanging heavy in the air. Now, added to the aroma of human waste and body odor was the cloying smell of oil and exhaust.

Guards armed with plastic pipes zigzagged through the plant, patrolling it, and continually shouting at the workers.

"Faster, go faster!" The guards screamed. If they didn't feel someone was working at their full capacity, they would strike out with their pipes, hitting and beating the women like cattle being urged to move quicker.

But the guards were not the workers only problem. There was also Kil Soo Lee. The plant owner would visit the factory floor on a regular basis, urging the guards to hit certain workers, and repeatedly telling them not to worry if they killed them because he would take full responsibility for it. When he wasn't ordering beatings, Lee was busy groping the women, squeezing their breasts, patting their buttocks, and rubbing his hands between their legs. Several times Lee would order women off the floor and take them away. When they returned, the women would be crying and upset, a look of shame evident on their faces. Many would later admit that their boss had forced them to have sex with him.

The work days were long, and the atmosphere on the factory floor was one of terror and despair. The workers were given barely anything to eat, and what they did receive was almost inedible. Kil Soo Lee fed all 313 employees on little more than three or four heads of cabbage boiled in water with a little musty rice thrown in for good measure. Only very rarely were they treated to a small bowl of chicken casserole.

As a result of these meager rations, everyone in the factory began losing weight at a rapid pace. Most were tiny Asian women to begin with, girls who couldn't afford to lose weight anyway. But that didn't matter, each of them got thinner and thinner until the factory looked like it was housing nothing more than a bunch of walking skeletons. After a while, many of the women were so malnourished and abused that they quit getting their monthly menstrual cycles. Everyone at Daewoosa, men as well as women, quickly became weak and frail within the first few months of arriving.

Beatings were one form of punishment, but starvation was another. Even though none of the employees got enough to eat, there were times when certain ones were denied any food for days at a time. Despite being in this weakened condition, the employees knew not to let their work load decrease or they risked a beating on top of their starvation.

The workers lived under constant threats of arrest, jail, and deportation, not to mention the $5,000 fine they would incur if they quit or broke the contract. Most couldn't have left even if they wanted to because Kil Soo Lee immediately confiscated all passports as soon as the workers arrived.

Sometimes, when it was too suffocating to stay inside, the workers would go outside to try and catch a breeze inside the enclosed fence of the compound. One Samoan man who lived nearby would find his heart breaking every time he saw the young women out there. Although he and others could never have imagined how truly awful things were for the Daewoosa workers, they were aware that they didn't have it easy inside those locked gates. The whole bunch of them appeared to be starving to death, and many of the women would cry at the fence begging for food. At other times, when the workers were allowed outside the factory gates, the islander's would see them in town ravaging through garbage cans looking for something to eat.

The Samoan man who lived nearby could not afford to feed the group, but he did try to make their life a little more bearable. Often, he would drive his truck over to the compound and park just outside of the fence. There, he would set up a movie screen in the bed of his pick-up truck, and using a movie projector he would show films to the mass of workers milling around outside. The man would stare at the workers as they watched the movie, and each time he did, he was reminded of pictures he had seen from WWII. To him, the workers looked just like Germany's Jews, with their gaunt and sad faces sitting atop emancipated bodies, peering out from behind the concentration camp fences.

****

Kil Soo Lee robbed his workers blind from the moment they began working for him. The minimum wage in American Samoa was $2.60 per hour, totaling a monthly salary of $460.00. Yet the most Lee ever paid anyone was $195.00 a month, and many of those who worked for him were paid nothing at all. If the workers questioned the amounts in their paycheck, Lee would explain that he had to deduct $200 a month for room and board, despite the fact that they had been told this would be free before they came. If they continued to question it, their inquiries would be met with a slap in the face or a hit from a plastic plumbing pipe.

The workers were despondent and afraid. Many had borrowed huge sums of money to come here, and now their families were left back home to deal with the consequences. Loan sharks were calling in loans, and some were threatening to take away people's houses if the money wasn't paid. Their families had no money to pay the debts, and the workers now had none to send to them.One evening after leaving the compound and going into town, several young female workers had come across the Seafarers Center, a shelter run by Christian missionaries in the city of Pago Pago. The center staff was kind to them and gave them some food to eat.

On the evening of Sunday, March 28, 1999, five of these girls returned to the center crying and upset, and begging for help. The girls did not speak English, and communicating was difficult for the center staff, but they were able to get the gist of what the girls were trying to tell them. They were hungry, the girls said, and had not eaten since Friday, two days earlier.

The missionaries fed the frightened Vietnamese, and tried to interpret what the girls so desperately wanted to tell them. From what they could gather, being deprived of food was a common punishment at the factory, and the workers stayed because they had no way leave. Not only had their employer confiscated everyone's passports but, despite the fact the girls had been working there since 1998, none of them had received any money at all.

Captain Rob Stip, an American missionary, on the island with his wife and son, was appalled by the girl's story and immediately called the U.S. Embassy in Washington D.C. The girls spoke to someone first, and then Stip got on the line with an Embassy official. When he finally hung up, the captain asked the Vietnamese if they could return the next day and bring a copy of the contract they had signed before coming to American Samoa. The girls agreed, and then quickly left the center.

But the next day, as Captain Stip waited for the girls to arrive, he received a call from an unidentified female saying the girls would not be coming because the factory was on lockdown. Later in the afternoon, around 5:30 pm, Stip received a second phone call, this time from a crying young girl who pleaded with him to come to the factory at once. Although the captain didn't know what was going on, he agreed to drive out there but decided to take another staff member, Kevin Moushon, with him.

When the two men arrived at the factory, they saw three or four girls sitting inside the security gate, several guards standing around them. As soon as the guards saw Stip and Moushon walking towards them, they began beating the helpless girls, hitting and kicking them brutally, as they pled for mercy and tried to ward off the blows.

Stip and Moushon were stunned by the savagery, and then they saw something that shocked them even more. Rushing towards the fence, covered in blood and bruises, were approximately 30 more young Vietnamese girls. Each of them were crying hysterically, and begging the two men to help them.

Stip and Moushon stared at each other for a moment, confused and baffled, and then the captain demanded to know what was going on.

But the guards refused to answer, and instead started beating the girls again, hitting, slapping, kicking and punching as the terrified workers tried to crawl away to escape the abuse. No one seemed to notice the big shiny car pull up and the large Samoan man exit it.

Moving to stand between the two men and the fence, the man glared at Stip and Moushon, and then identified himself as an attorney representing the Daewoosa Garment Factory. He ordered the men to leave immediately and threatened to call the police if they didn't.

A furious Captain Stip told the attorney to go ahead and call the police, as he had no intention of going anywhere until he was told why the girls were being beaten.

The attorney called Stip's bluff and within minutes police officer David Snow arrived. He tried to calm things down and then, incredibly, he ordered the two men to leave the premises immediately. Stip and Moushon began to protest, trying to explain to the officer what was happening to the young girls, but Snow cut them off. He had already spoken to the factory owner, Kil Soo Lee, Snow told them, and he had explained everything. The girls were 'hysterical' Lee claimed, because he had punished them by withholding their food. He denied that he had every abused the girls, or 'watched them dress or take a shower.'

Stip and Moushon stared at the officer open-mouthed. Who had said anything about watching the girls dress or take a shower, they wondered? Just what in the hell was actually going on in this factory? But neither man got the opportunity to ask any questions. Officer Snow insisted they leave right now or he was going to arrest both of them. Stip and Moushon felt they had little choice. They couldn't help anyone if they were sitting behind bars so the two men reluctantly departed from the factory.

Both Captain Stip and Kevin Moushon returned to the Seafarers Center angry, upset and worried. Worse yet, Stip and his family were scheduled to fly back home to North Carolina that very evening, and would not be returning for an entire month. The captain hated to go, especially now, but the plans had already been made and the plane tickets bought weeks ago. There was not much he could do about it.

Kevin Moushon was left in charge of the center during the Captain's absence, and two days after Stip returned home, he received a call from him. Moushon told him that one of the girls from the factory had run away and was at the center now.

"What should I do?" Moushon asked.

Stip wasn't sure what he should tell him. After the fiasco with Officer Dave Snow he certainly wasn't going to suggest he call the police. Nor did he think the girl should return to the factory, where he feared she might be killed this time. Captain Stip felt agitated and useless. He was 10,000 miles away, how was he supposed to know what to do?

Finally, the Captain told Moushon to give the girl refuge and help her in any way he could. He didn't know what else to say.

****

One week after Captain Stip left American Samoa, two more Daewoosa workers showed up at the Seafarers Center in the wee hours of the morning. This time it was two young Vietnamese men who were fluent in English. The men had risked their lives to leave, having snuck out of the compound and scaled the razor wire fence after hearing about the center from some of the other workers.

This time, those at the center heard the entire story of life behind the locked gates of the Daewoosa Garment Factory and the poor workers who were at the mercy of Kil Soo Lee. They listened in shocked silence as the story tumbled out of the two terrified men.

They heard about beatings and abuse, threats of arrest and deportation, the confiscated passports, starvation, and the fear those locked inside lived with every day. They were told of women being sexually harassed and raped, of 18 hour work days for little or no pay, of filthy and unsanitary conditions, and of Samoan guards who brutalized the workers.

It was a shocking story indeed, but not that surprising. Those at the center had not forgotten the other terrified workers, or what Captain Stip and Kevin Moushon had seen. The center was run by missionaries, Christian people who had dedicated their lives to helping others. Each of those working there knew that something needed to be done to help the workers at the Daewoosa Garment Factory.

So once again workers at the Seafarer Center placed a call to the U.S. Embassy, but this time they placed a second call as well, to a local civil rights attorney living on the island.

The two workers met with the lawyer and once again repeated their story of life at the factory. After much discussion, and some investigation, the attorney convinced a handful of workers to file a civil suit against Kil Soo Lee for their back wages.

Finally, the lawsuit was enough to bring some attention to the factory, and in May the U.S. Department of Labor, (DPL), and the National Labor Relations Board, (NLRB), began an investigation of the South Korean factory owner.

The suit was met with displeasure from both the Vietnamese and the American Samoan governments. It was embarrassing, and brought attention to each that they didn't want. On American Samoa, it also threatened to harm their tourism trade.

But no one was as unhappy as Kil Soo Lee, who was absolutely irate about the whole thing. He ordered his workers to drop their cases against him, but it was already too late. Even if his employees did agree to drop the case, the United States government was already involved, and everyone knew that although the wheels of government might turn slowly, once they were in motion they were almost impossible to stop.

Lee had other problems he was dealing with at the same time. He was upset to find that the lawsuit seemed to infuse his workers with courage they had not previously shown. They were calling their families, and smuggling letters of complaint out of the factory to mail to them. One girl had sent her father a heartbreaking letter of life on American Samoa, and the foolish man had actually gone to the Vietnamese authorities over it.

The girl's father had first visited the Ministry of Education Works and then the State Department, who in turn had sent him to the director of Tourism. The Vietnamese reaction to this 'troublemaker' at the Daewoosa Factory is evidenced by the father's reply to his daughter:

'We were reprimanded, [by the director of tourism],*' the man wrote. 'There I was told you and 16 other workers went on strike for something about wages being early or late, I don't know. Why would you do that to bring shame on our family? I feel if you do not work according to the terms you and I have signed with the company, I am afraid you will be a pawn on the chessboard. On the other hand, you should not think the other 16 workers are all good people. Who knows, maybe they need to eliminate a pawn? About your life, I implore you to obey the leadership and the organization. There is no other way.'*

But the civil suit had shaken Lee, and he was beginning to fear that he might lose complete control of his workers. The last thing he needed was more attention being focused on his factory. He began keeping the Daewoosa compound on lockdown more often than not these days.

Frightened as he might be, when the DPL completed their investigation and levied fines against him in the amount of $755,000, Lee still chose to ignore them. Publicity of not, Kil Soo Lee was loath to part with any of his money. When the DPL also ordered him to start paying back wages owed to his employees, Lee pled poverty, claiming he had no money to do so.

If he was worried about defying the United States government, he didn't show it. In fact, Lee acted as if nothing had happened, and things continued at the Daewoosa factory just as they had always been. When no repercussions were forthcoming after his failure to comply with the DPL and NLRB demands, Lee relaxed even more.

Although the DPL would have liked to shut the Daewoosa factory down and put Kil Soo Lee out of business, they had no authority to do so. And when the factory owner failed to pay his workers the back wages that were owed them, the DPL and the NLRB issued his employees the checks themselves.

On the very day his workers received those checks, some in the amount of $2500 and more, Kil Soo Lee confiscated each and deposited them into his personal checking account. Any worker who balked at turning the money over was immediately scheduled for deportation.

When he took these checks to the American Samoan bank, Lee paid a visit to a loan officer and attempted to bribe him into authorizing a $500,000 loan he had recently applied for.

Nothing had come of the investigations and the lawsuit, and Lee's legal troubles seemed to be behind him. But the anger he harbored over what his workers had done was just beginning. From that moment on, conditions in the factory grew even worse. The beatings increased, and the workers were watched more closely. The compound was often on lockdown now and no one was allowed to leave. Lee had no intention of letting anyone else seek help at any shelters. The workers were absolutely miserable, and at night they sobbed in their sleep. One woman would later say about this time; "It sounded like everyone was going insane."

****

The factory workers considered the civil suit a failure, and were depressed that little seemed to come from it, other than harsher living conditions. They had no idea that, although it might have appeared to generate little publicity for them, behind the scenes it had gotten things moving. The suit brought the plight of the workers to the attention of the U.S. government and the people on American Samoa. And by the end of the year, the internet would bring it to the attention of the entire world.

One person who read about what was happening at the garment factory on the South Pacific Island was Hai-Tri Le, a Vietnam War refugee living in the United States. Le had made a good life for himself after the war, settling in the Seattle Washington area and securing an impressive position with The Microsoft Corporation. He was appalled by what he was reading and hearing concerning his fellow countrymen on American Samoa, and he was determined to help them in any way he could.

Someone else who was keeping an eye on what was happening on American Samoa was Representative Chris Smith, a Republican from the state of New Jersey. One of Smith's key aides had lived on the island and was familiar with the factory. Smith was a real humanitarian who was sickened by today's world of human trafficking and modern day slavery. He had been working tirelessly on ways to end these despicable practices, and he would eventually be the prime sponsor in getting the Trafficking Victims Protection Act passed later that year. It was a law that would play a big part in the fate of Kil Soo Lee, but it wouldn't prevent one of the most vicious occurrences from happening at his factory.

Chapter Three

Shortly after the Human Trafficking Victims Protection Law was passed on October 28, 2000, the Daewoosa Samoa Garment Factory received a large order from JC Penney. The order was on a time limit, and needed to be completed within a month. Rush orders were always daunting tasks, and they always raised the stress level in the factory considerably, but Kil Soo Lee was determined to fulfill this one.

Things had been tense at Daewoosa for months. Between the legal troubles, the passing of the anti-trafficking law, and now the pressure of fulfilling this rush order, it seemed everyone's nerves were frazzled. Kil Soo Lee was stressed, the Samoan guards who prowled the factory floors were anxious, and the weary workers were apprehensive.

On November 28, 2000, despite the fact that it was late fall, the weather on the island of American Samoa was brutal. The sun was blazing hot, the air heavy with humidity, sticky, cloying, and nearly suffocating. Inside the corrugated metal confines of the Daewoosa Garment Factory, the temperature soared to 104 degrees. The workers sweated heavily, their hair and clothing so wet with perspiration they might have just stepped out of a shower.

The guards zigzagging amongst the workers, glaring menacingly and keeping their plastic pipes at the ready. All of the guards were Samoan, but not all of them were men. Lee often used female guards as well, and they could be every bit as vicious as their male counterparts. But the females were not employed for security, most were workers on the line who would only be pulled from their machines when needed.

On this day, the 30 guards roaming the factory floor were all men, each weighing between 200 and 300 pounds, and the tension in the room was palpable. The pressure to fulfill the JC Penney contract, combined with the stifling conditions inside the building, had everyone feeling more stressful and miserable than ever.

Daewoosa Samoa was fashioned in an assembly line, with each article of clothing moving from worker to worker, as different alterations were made. Those at the beginning of the line started immediately, but those at the end had no work until the assembly line began to move steadily.

Dung Nguyen sat next to 21-year-old Truong Thi Le Quyon, another Vietnamese seamstress who occupied the sewing machine next to hers. Dung was not feeling well. The heat, combined with the lack of food, made her feel weak and faint. The two women were at the end of the line, sitting at their sewing machines, waiting for the work to reach them.

Lee was on the floor too, urging his workers to move faster, shouting at them continuously. Dung watched as one of the Samoan guards approached her and Truong and began screaming at them about 'not working.' Truong tried to explain that the assembly line had not yet reached them, but the guard would not be pacified. Soon, Kil Soo Lee had moved over to the small group and joined his guard.

The two women were trying to explain the situation, but Lee and the guard were hearing none of it. Suddenly, the guard grabbed Truong by the hair and pulled her from her chair. He wrapped his massive hands around her delicate neck, and began squeezing the life out of her. Dung, thinking he would kill the woman, began to scream. She watched as Truong's eyes bulged in terror, and saw her face turn from pink to red to blue. Other workers stopped to stare at the altercation, some of them beginning to rise from their own seats.

Two Vietnamese men rushed to the guard and tried to interfere, and then, according to Dung, "it all happened." The guard released his grip on Truong long enough to begin clubbing the Vietnamese men with his plastic pipe. When other guards hurried over and took over the beating, the original guard turned back to Truong who was lying on the floor gasping for air. Immediately, he began beating on her, striking her in the head and the body, as she tried to pull herself into a fetal position.

Kil Soo Lee stood among them, smiling with glee and screaming at the top of his lungs. "Don't worry if you kill her," he shouted, "I'll take the blame for it."

The guard, egged on by his boss, grabbed Truong around the neck again and began dragging her towards the factory doors. He pulled her between the rows of the assembly line, leaving a trail of blood in his wake, as the other workers shouted for him to stop.

Suddenly, one Vietnamese man, Nguyen Thai Quang ran towards the two and grabbed hold of Truong, trying to pull her back. Other guards descended on him, clubbing him in the face and head, knocking out several of his teeth, and rupturing his eardrum. Other workers came to his rescue, but they were assaulted themselves, and soon the entire factory floor was in an all-out brawl.

There was fighting and screaming and yelling between everyone. Over and over again the guards raised their plastic pipes and brought them down on the Vietnamese and Chinese workers. Blood sprayed the entire factory, landing on the floor, the machines, and the garments, covering everything with a layer of crimson gore.

Outside the factory doors there was more fighting. The guard had managed to get Truong outside, but other Vietnamese had followed him, and other guards had followed them. There was an entire melee inside and out. Sialavaa Fagaima, a sometime seamstress who also worked as a security guard in the factory, picked up a plastic pipe and began swinging herself.

Fagaima hit and clubbed and beat any worker who came within range. So violently did she swing that she shattered the pipe she was holding, leaving its end jagged and splintered, turning it into a sinister and deadly weapon. Soon, Fagaima turned her lethal pipe onto Truong. She beat the woman mercilessly about the face and head, until one of those splintered ends caught the terrified woman perfectly at the corner of her eye. The jagged piece of plastic continued to move, gouging into the eye socket, entering Truong's head, and bringing her eyeball out with it when Fagaima finally pulled it back.

The sight was like something out of a horror movie. The blood gushed profusely out of the open wound, and the eyeball, now triple the size it appears when resting in the eye socket, dangled down below Truong's face held fast by a bloody and grotesque vein attached somewhere deep within her head.

Truong began to scream and react, clasping her hands over her gushing eye socket she blundered forward in a blind panic of fear and pain. Every time she moved, she sprayed and showered the gathering crowd with droplets of scarlet colored blood. Finally, the sight of her seemed to wake everybody up and the fighting quickly came to an end. The guards were scared, it was obvious that this time the beatings had gone too far.

They carried the injured woman back inside, where the sight of her brought an immediate halt to the others fighting on the factory floor. The woman was covered with blood, and Dung could see that she was badly hurt. It looked like a massacre had taken place inside the building, with almost every inch of it covered in a fine red mist.

The workers were immediately ordered back to their dormitories where they huddled in groups, terrified and afraid. In all the confusion of the melee, several workers had managed to leave the compound and were in town calling their families, begging for help to get back home. Everyone wanted to leave American Samoa right then and there.

But there was little their families could do.

****

Back on the factory floor, those workers who were too injured to be sent to the dormitories, including Truong Thi Le Quyon and Nguyen Thai Quang, lay on the ground in a heap. Some of the guards were trying to help them, but Kil Soo Lee didn't seem concerned, in fact he seemed enraged. He had an order to fill, damn it, and he had thousands of dollars of ruined, blood covered garments, and no workers on the floor.

While the injured lay helpless, Kil Soo Lee ranted and raved for two entire hours before the guards finally convinced him that they needed to go for help. Only then did Lee allow his workers to be taken to a hospital. But he made sure that the hospital staff was told that the workers had begun to riot, and the injuries were 'accidents' that occurred while the guards were trying to protect themselves.

Later that night, Virginia Soliai, a manager in the factory, visited the workers in their dormitories and ordered them to back up the story. She insisted that they file false reports indicating that any injuries suffered were incurred as a result of self-defense.

****

Kil Soo Lee had finally calmed down and begun to assess his situation, and for the first time ever, the South Korean businessman was truly scared. He doubted he could sweep this incident under the rug as neatly as he had the civil suit and the DPL investigation, and he quickly began making plans to secure his future. During the month of December, Lee visited several banks on the island of American Samoa.

Kil Soo Lee had been right. This time, things would not be swept under the rug so easily, and on January 12, 2001, a Samoan court ordered the Daewoosa Garment Factory into receivership. The factory had been a lucrative business, having exported over 8 million dollars in goods during some months, but despite this fact, the receiver found the company's bank accounts with a balance of only $538.00. Lee's many visits to the banks had enabled him to withdraw hundreds of thousands of dollars in the days and weeks leading up to the receivership. It seemed apparent now that Daewoosa Samoa Garment Factory LTD was bankrupt.

****

For more than a year now, Hai-Tri Le, the Microsoft employee back in Seattle, had been trying to bring the plight of the Daewoosa workers into the public eye. He had contacted many organizations, including SOS Boat People and the National Labor Committee, two humanitarian rights groups, and everyone was just as concerned as him. But getting the public, or the government, to come forward and take a stand had not occurred.

Now, upon hearing about the latest happening at the factory, Hai-Tri Le decided he needed to do something drastic to bring attention to the horrors being perpetrated on the island of American Samoa.

In February, Le took a leave of absence from Microsoft, traveled to American Samoa, and infiltrated the factory. For ten days, he bunked in the men's dormitory and worked on the factory floor, documenting everything he saw, and heard, with notes and pictures taken on his digital camera.

When he finally returned home, Le and several others took their case to the public in full force. They had been pressuring the United States Department of Justice to do something about the factory since 1999, with no luck. But now, armed with evidence that could blow the entire scandal sky high, the FBI took notice. And in late February of 2001, they finally travelled to American Samoa and began an investigation.

But they had not moved fast enough. The Daewoosa fiasco had been tremendously embarrassing to the Vietnam government, and they were determined to keep their role in it from being made public. Because of the FBI's failure to become involved earlier, a Vietnam Labor Company Official was able to fly to American Samoa and pressure his people to return home, and several did.

On March 23, 2001, the FBI arrested Kil Soo Lee on American Samoa and charged him with involuntary servitude and false labor practices. The disgraced businessman was immediately flown to the state of Hawaii and placed in a jail cell to await trial.

Although the Daewoosa Samoa Garment Factory was officially closed down, its workers were allowed to remain in the dormitories where they lived alone and virtually penniless. They had no way to return home and most were too afraid to go anyway. Not only were they terrified of the retribution they might suffer because of their association with the factory, but they were still responsible for the large debts they had incurred and they had no way to pay them back.

While the ex-workers wondered what would become of them, they struggled to find a way to get food and survive. They roamed the towns knocking on stranger's doors, and asking churches and shelters for help. Many offered to work in exchange for food, and were grateful to accept any odd job; sewing, cleaning, babysitting and running errands.

Some of the Samoans residents were kind and generous, paying the workers well for their efforts. But others were more than happy to take advantage of the situation, promising to pay but never coming through with the money. It was a sad situation all around.

Chapter Four

If the former workers from the Daewoosa Factory were despondent over the circumstances that had befallen their lives, they would have been grateful to know they had a champion in their corner. Hai-Tri Le had been fighting for their cause for more than a year now, and his drive and determination to help his fellow countrymen was intense and furious.

Le had spent copious amounts of money, risked his life and his job, and rarely saw his family in his quest to save those who fell victim to Kil Soo Lee. It was he who was instrumental in involving other human rights groups to join in pressuring the justice department to act, and it was he who was still working with them.

The Justice Department finally informed Le that Vietnam had plans to repatriate their former Daewoosa workers, and intended to send an airplane to American Samoa to bring them home. Le feared that those who returned to Vietnam would face political retribution, and he inquired about the United States granting citizenship to the refugees. But the Justice Department was reluctant to offer residency to such a large number of people, and they told Le, tentatively, that they might be willing to grant sanctuary to 20 former workers if they agreed to testify against Kil Soo Lee.

Hai-Tri Le was confused and angry. The Justice Departments offer simply wasn't good enough. Le believed that all the former employees should be allowed to come to the United States since all of them had endured the same hardships and abuse, and he was not about to just let the matter rest. Joining forces with dozens of volunteers and a handful of attorney's, Le and his group fought to gain U.S. residency for every former factory worker.

The United States, Le claimed, could easily do this, and in fact, had an obligation to under the new 'T' Immigration Visa, which provided sanctuary to federal witnesses who helped prosecute human traffickers and smugglers. The publicity worked, and as the general public rallied behind Le and the others, the Justice Department finally agreed.

They would give residency to those immigrants who had suffered at the hands of Kil Soo Lee and his Daewoosa Factory, but there was still another problem. The department didn't have the staff to find homes, sponsors and airline tickets for the stranded immigrants. Le and the others were not discouraged however. If the Justice Department couldn't do it, they would do it themselves.

This may have been easier said than done though, once the group found out about the time crunch they were on. The Vietnamese plane was due to arrive on American Samoa in as little as two weeks. Those trying to help the former factory workers would have only 10 days to accomplish their mission.

Hai-Tri Le immediately took another leave of absence from Microsoft and got on the internet and the phones. He created websites, posting messages that read: Your Fellow Vietnamese Need Your Help! He and dozens of others made phone calls to attorneys, the Justice Department, travel agents, churches, shelters, and anyone else they could think of. Le's cell phone bill alone ran $3,000 for the month.

Within days, 600 people had volunteered to help. But time was running out, and now, when Le placed phone calls, he had no time for questions or explanations. His manner was abrupt and to the point.

"Can you take workers? How many? Do you know of any other jobs for them? Do you know of any place that would sponsor them? Shelter them? Help them? Are you a Church? A business? A philanthropist? What?"

Finally, when their time was up, Le realized that there were still many, many workers left on the South Pacific Island. But he had made a promise to these people, and he intended to keep it. Le, and two volunteers, purchased each of the former workers a one way ticket off of American Samoa themselves. The cost to these three individuals was a staggering $42,000, of which $25,000 was charged to Le's credit card alone.

Now, with airline tickets in hand, Le found there were other problems. Some of the Vietnamese didn't want to go, they wanted to return home. They missed their families, and many husbands were adamant that their wives come back. The women were crying, torn between what they should do. They wanted to be with their husbands, who were threatening divorce, a shameful fate for a Vietnamese woman, but they were afraid to go home. They vacillated on what they should do, frustrating everyone involved.

As bad as that was, Le found it even worse that some of the former workers could not be found. They were still living in the dormitories, and doing work for island natives and no one knew whether they were working or looking for wages that were owed to them. Le found out that many of the Samoans they worked for had promised to pay them at the airport, and when they didn't show up, the former workers went looking for them. One Vietnamese girl missed her plane because she was trying to hunt down people who owed her $10.00, despite the fact that her missed plane ticket had cost $800. Le would be thankful when everyone was finally standing upon U.S. soil.

Things were difficult for the former workers when they first reached America, but nowhere near as difficult as it was for those who were repatriated back to Vietnam. For them, life was unbelievably hard and cruel back in their own country. Creditors hounded them daily, and several ex-workers had to go into hiding to avoid them. Twenty families lost their homes to loan sharks when they couldn't repay their debts. Those who had worked at Daewoosa were constantly ordered to report to the police to answer questions about their experiences on American Samoa, and many couldn't find jobs because they were now ostracized by their fellow countrymen. They wrote heartbreaking letters to the United States government, pleading with them for help since their own government refused to do so.

A lot of people who had read about what they had experienced wanted to help, and many wrote letters on their behalf to the U.S. government too. A church in Hawaii held a fund raiser and took up a collection to purchase Truong Thi Le Quyen a new glass eye. Others contributed to help pay for the surgery it would take to have the eye implanted. Countless others would have liked to help, but they really didn't know what they could do.

****

In August, Kil Soo Lee was indicted on 22 counts including involuntary servitude, extortion, money laundering, false financial reporting and bribery of a bank official. Also indicted with him were four others: Virginia Soliai and Robert Atimalala, two factory supervisors accused of working in concert with Samoan officials to deport workers who complained, Elekana Nuuuli Ioane, another factory supervisor who was accused of carrying out the beatings ordered by Kil Soo Lee, and Sialavaa Fagaima, the security guard who gouged out Truong's eye. Each was charged with human trafficking among other things.

Before Lee's trial even began, Ioane and Fagaima both pled guilty to the charges leveled against them. Fagaima received a sentence of 4 years and 3 months, while Ioane received 5 years 10 months. Both expressed remorse for their actions at sentencing.

Fagaima, looking meek and docile as she cried before the court, told the Judge, "There has never been a day or a night when I have forgotten what I have done. I wish I could turn it back, but I can't."

Ione, whispering in a soft voice, simply told the court, "I just want to say sorry. What I did was wrong."

Kil Soo Lee, the man ultimately responsible for all of this, never showed any remorse or sorrow at all.

Afterword

Kil Soo Lee went to trial on October 22, 2002 before U.S. District Judge Susan Oki Mollway in Honolulu Hawaii. Originally charged with twenty-two counts, by this time four of them had been dismissed, but Lee still faced the possibility of conviction on eighteen separate counts. Also being tried alongside him were Robert Atimalala, and Virginia Soliai.

Twenty-one former Daewoosa employee's testified to the mistreatment they were subjected to at the hands of the one-time respected businessman. Some of those who took the stand were former supervisors and guards who drastically downplayed their participation in the horrors that occurred in the factory. For four entire months the trial dragged on slowly, but on February 21, 2003 Kil Soo Lee was convicted on 14 of the 18 counts. The jury judged that he was guilty of conspiracy, extortion, money laundering and 11 counts of involuntary servitude. Robert Atimalala and Virginia Soliai were subsequently found not guilty.

Lee's sentencing was delayed repeatedly for several different reasons, including the firing of his one-time attorney. When he appeared in court with his lawyer on January 28, 2004, Lee appeared glassy-eyed and confused. His attorney asked for another delay, claiming that he could no longer communicate with his client. When Judge Mollway tried to speak to Lee and ask him questions, the former factory owner simply stared at her shaking his head. He didn't understand the proceedings he repeatedly told her.

The Judge, although skeptical of Lee's newfound stupidity, had little choice but to postpone the hearing. She ordered Lee to undergo a mental evaluation, and scheduled a new sentencing date of May 6, 2004. But it was not until more than a year later, on June 22, 2005, that Kil Soo Lee was finally sentenced for his part in the happenings at the Daewoosa Samoa Garment Factory. Lee received a total of 40 years in prison, and was ordered to pay 1.8 million dollars in restitution.

The former factory owner's attorney immediately appealed on the grounds that Lee should not have been tried on United States soil but instead in American Samoa. The high court however, ruled that American Samoa did not have the courts to try him, and that the United States had jurisdiction for these types of federal crimes.

Today, Lee is 63-years-old and remains behind bars. It is likely he will die in prison. His Daewoosa factory has been shut down and remains a sad embarrassment for the island of American Samoa.

A total of 272 former Daewoosa workers now live in the United States, thanks to hundreds of people like Hai-Tri Le. Although they are scattered throughout the U.S., several of the women live in the Seattle area. For some, it is a new life with a bright future, but for others, it is a sad and lonely existence.

Many of the single women have found new loves in America and are starting new families. Others were eventually reunited with husbands and children, who were left in Vietnam, when they also qualified for residency in the United States. For them, the future looks bright too.

But for many more, there remains only memories of past lives, and loneliness in a foreign country filled with strangers. To these women, those they love remain in Vietnam, either unable or unwilling to start a new life thousands of miles away. Dung Nguyen is one of them. She lives alone in Seattle, working twelve hours a day, six days a week. She welcomes the long hours; they keep her from thinking too much.

Hai-Tri Le keeps in touch with those he helped to rescue from American Samoa, and they dream of the day all the former factory workers will be reunited with their families. To the ex-Daewoosa employees, Le is a hero of the greatest kind.

The two Vietnamese men who scaled the fence at the factory and sought help from the Seafarer Center have completely vanished. The Samoan government has stated that the two were victims of a drowning accident, but former factory workers have denounced this explanation. Their whereabouts remain unknown.

JC Penney, and many of the other large department stores that purchased clothing from the Daewoosa Garment Factory, immediately canceled their contracts with the distributor who supplied them. All of the garments from the factory were eventually auctioned off.

Lawyers from American Samoa and the United States filed a lawsuit against Kil Soo Lee, and two Vietnamese Labor Offices, for the employees of the garment factory. Eventually, an American Samoa court awarded the former workers 3.5 million dollars in damages. But since Lee is bankrupt, and sitting in prison, none of his ex-employees have seen a dime, and they are not ever likely too. Many are fighting to have the Vietnamese government pay, since they were judged responsible along with Lee, but so far nothing has come of that either.

What happened at the Daewoosa Samoa Garment Factory was undoubtedly a tragedy, and the conditions its workers were forced to live in were brutal and cruel. But not more so than thousands of other 'sweatshops' operating throughout the world. Had Kil Soo Lee not chosen an American territory to open his factory, chances are good that it would still be in operation today.

Perhaps one day more attention will be focused on those who find themselves working and living in sweatshops, and stricter penalties enforced on those who operate them. But since human trafficking is an enterprise that generates 7 to 10 billion dollars in profit each year, the greed of many will most likely keep that from ever happening. For it is only when each and every country takes a stand against such modern day slavery that anything might be accomplished in the fight to end it.

Bibliography

http://archives.starbulletin.com/2001/09/05/news/story10.html

http://www.globallabourrights.org/reports?id=0215

http://www.seattlepi.com/default/article/Chapter-1-Servitude-in-American-Samoa-1129763.php#page-3

http://www.justice.gov/opa/pr/2003/February/03_crt_108.htm

http://www.nytimes.com/2002/05/10/opinion/sweatshops-under-the-american-flag.html

http://www.seattlepi.com/default/article/The-story-behind-the-story-1129932.php

http://www.seattlepi.com/default/article/Sentencing-delayed-for-garment-factory-owner-1135848.php

http://www.seattlepi.com/default/article/Chapter-4-Smiles-laughter-and-a-wedding-in-a-1130067.php

http://www.seattlepi.com/default/article/A-joyful-reunion-for-woman-who-escaped-cruelty-of-1134873.php

http://www.seattlepi.com/default/article/Acts-of-kindness-showered-on-sweatshop-workers-1130378.php

http://www.seattlepi.com/default/article/The-U-S-acted-too-slowly-some-say-1130042.php

http://www.seattlepi.com/default/article/Chapter-3-Dramatic-flurry-rescues-workers-1130041.php

http://www.seattlepi.com/default/article/Timeline-1130039.php

http://www.seattlepi.com/default/article/In-her-own-words-Christa-Lin-attorney-for-1129988.php

http://www.seattlepi.com/default/article/The-story-behind-the-story-1129932.php

http://www.seattlepi.com/news/article/In-her-own-words-Dung-Nguyen-1129766.php

http://www.seattlepi.com/default/article/In-his-own-words-I-implore-you-to-obey-the-1130056.php

www.dfat.gov.au/geo/american_samoa/american_samoa.brief.html

http://econlib.org/library/Columns/y2008/Powellsweatshops.html

http://www.ilr.cornell.edu/trianglefire/

www.mzi.com/pages/news.php?op=read&id=3744

http://archive.starbulletin.com/2004/02/02/news/story11.html

Northwest Florida Daily News 09/02/01